Independent Thinking on Resto force in restorative working. Pra ligent, this book is crucial for relational approach to teaching

Mark Finnis is quite simply the don of restorative practice.

**PAUL DIX, BEHAVIOUR SPECIALIST,
WHENTHEADULTSCHANGE.COM**

I adore the fact that one of the first things Mark addresses in this book is the 'L word' – love – and that in our school communities we need to 'spread it thick, like my mum spreads butter'.

He uses strong evidence to show that when schools use restorative practice effectively, both attendance and attainment improve. This is no woolly idea, and he provides a cohesive strategy for changing schools towards becoming relational. A happy, well respected child is a child who can learn and engage.

In these times of isolating pupils, he shows us that the way to reduce negative behaviours and communication is inclusion over exclusion and problem-solving over punishment. However, he doesn't share a one-size-fits-all mentality here; instead he offers a plethora of fantastic ideas to build this change.

His writing is quite simply a groundbreaking dive into the importance of social capital, relationships, humanity and compassion – in fact all the things that we know bring out the best in a whole community.

Independent Thinking on Restorative Practice is a compelling and articulate read, and by the end you are brimming with ideas and love.

**CHRIS DYSON, HEAD TEACHER,
PARKLANDS PRIMARY SCHOOL**

For far too long the education world has needed a thorough, authentic and expert guide to restorative practice, written by someone who really knows their stuff – and here it is!

In *Independent Thinking on Restorative Practice* Mark Finnis harnesses his years of experience to bring us the perfect balance of theory and practical advice. He is a true champion of relational practice and shows us how values and cultural development can lead to strong relationships and therefore positive behaviour, of both adults and children.

If you truly want to embrace relationships as the heartbeat of your school culture, then this book will show you how. This really is a book to change hearts and minds.

DAVE WHITAKER, DIRECTOR OF LEARNING, WELLSPRING ACADEMY TRUST

This must-read book is the perfect balance of the principles and theory underpinning restorative practice and relational leadership – and it is peppered beautifully with practical examples of how to make it happen. Mark's warmth, humour and non-judgemental manner is palpable throughout, and his writing serves up a 'chicken soup for the soul'.

We will definitely be buying *Independent Thinking on Restorative Practice* for all our MAT's leaders.

KATE DAVIES, CEO, WHITE WOODS PRIMARY ACADEMY TRUST

Mark's common sense is remarkably uncommon. Detailing the 'why?', sharing the 'how?' and evidencing the impact, in *Independent Thinking on Restorative Practice* he takes you through working restoratively in a way that leaves you wondering why you didn't do it sooner and why you didn't read the book quicker! Mark's personal style of high challenge and high support echoes in dulcet Liverpudlian tones from every page of the book, provoking you to consider your leadership style, your values and what you really want to achieve.

> **LUCIE LAKIN, PRINCIPAL, CARR MANOR COMMUNITY SCHOOL, EXECUTIVE HEAD TEACHER, WETHERBY HIGH SCHOOL**

Part personal, part theory, part practical application, *Independent Thinking on Restorative Practice* is an eminently readable and always inspiring reminder of the power of working 'with'. Writing with passion, humour and enthusiasm, Mark has successfully managed to capture the essence of restorative practice he so expertly and inspiringly talks about at his training events. While the content is primarily focused through an education/school lens, the theory and practice described in the book is equally applicable across all disciplines.

If you are new to restorative practice, this book is a great place to start as a welcome and timely introduction to restorative practice from one of the UK's leading trainers. If you are someone who is more familiar with the subject, this is a really helpful 'go to' reminder that you can dip in and out of for inspiration.

> **NIGEL RICHARDSON, CBE, FORMER DIRECTOR OF CHILDREN'S SERVICES, LEEDS CITY COUNCIL**

Restorative practice is not simply a way of doing; it's a way of being, and it takes practice! In *Independent Thinking on Restorative Practice* Mark sets out key principles and their application, as well as the opportunities and challenges around their use, in this accessible, easy-to-read book. Furthermore, this book is not just for teachers – because restorative practice is not just for schools. It works for children, young people and families in a wide variety of contexts and settings, with young and old, with peers and colleagues, and in our work as leaders and managers.

In short, anyone interested in the power of human relationships to enable change to happen will find material in this book to help them.

ANDY COULDRICK, CHIEF EXECUTIVE,
BIRMINGHAM CHILDREN'S TRUST

In this book Mark Finnis guides the reader through restorative practice with clarity, insight, real-life examples and clear direction. It is full of practical ideas and advice on how to build relationships and create a restorative ethos at whole-school and classroom level.

Mark's words inspire courage and a belief that small changes will have a huge impact. Restorative approaches are not just for resolving conflict, and this book suggests many ways in which it can be built into day-to-day interactions throughout a school. Restorative practice is not a 'soft' or easy option, and the structures suggested in this book guide the reader through its many functions and possibilities.

Mark describes the challenges and successes of restorative practice with honesty and gentle humour, sharing his rich experiences in these approaches. The value of strong relationships underpins every chapter, empowering educators to build trust and reciprocity across their school community.

For any teacher or school leader, this is the handbook you are looking for on restorative practice.

JENNIFER M. KNUSSEN, HEAD TEACHER,
PITTEUCHAR EAST PRIMARY SCHOOL

INDEPENDENT THINKING ON …

RESTORATIVE PRACTICE

Mark Finnis

BUILDING RELATIONSHIPS, IMPROVING BEHAVIOUR
AND CREATING STRONGER COMMUNITIES

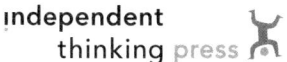

First published by

Independent Thinking Press
Crown Buildings, Bancyfelin, Carmarthen, Wales, SA33 5ND, UK
www.independentthinkingpress.com

and

Independent Thinking Press
PO Box 2223, Williston, VT 05495, USA
www.crownhousepublishing.com

Independent Thinking Press is an imprint of Crown House Publishing Ltd.

© Mark Finnis, 2021

The right of Mark Finnis to be identified as the author of this work has been asserted by him in accordance with the Copyright, Designs and Patents Act 1988.

First published 2021. Reprinted 2021 (three times), 2022, 2023.

All rights reserved. Except as permitted under current legislation no part of this work may be photocopied, stored in a retrieval system, published, performed in public, adapted, broadcast, transmitted, recorded or reproduced in any form or by any means, without the prior permission of the copyright owners. Enquiries should be addressed to Independent Thinking Press.

Pages 51 and 53, adapted from the social discipline window from T. Wachtel and P. McCold, Restorative Justice in Everyday Life in *Restorative Justice and Civil Society* © H. Strang and J. Braithwaite (eds), Cambridge University Press. Reproduced with permission of the Licensor through PLSclear.

Independent Thinking Press has no responsibility for the persistence or accuracy of URLs for external or third-party websites referred to in this publication, and does not guarantee that any content on such websites is, or will remain, accurate or appropriate.

Quotes from Ofsted and Department for Education documents used in this publication have been approved under an Open Government Licence. Please see: http://www.nationalarchives.gov.uk/doc/open-government-licence/version/3/.

Edited by Ian Gilbert.

The Independent Thinking On … series is typeset in Azote, Buckwheat TC Sans, Cormorant Garamond and Montserrat.

The Independent Thinking On … series cover style was designed by Tania Willis
www.taniawillis.com.

British Library Cataloguing-in-Publication Data
A catalogue entry for this book is available from the British Library.

Print ISBN 978-178135338-7
Mobi ISBN 978-178135389-9
ePub ISBN 978-178135390-5
ePDF ISBN 978-178135391-2

LCCN 2021931546

Printed and bound in the UK by
Gomer Press Llandysul, Ceredigion

I'd like to dedicate this book to my mum, who showed me what unconditional love is, who let me experience what it's like to have a champion in my corner and who always believed in me. Thanks from the bottom of my heart for everything you've done for me. I let you know how much I appreciate you as often as I can; this is me letting everyone else know too.

FOREWORD

In 2005 we had a significant piece of work ahead of us but also a great opportunity. The school, run-down and spread across two sites, was in recovery from a difficult period and, against the odds, had been thrown a lifeline. We were to have a brand new building.

We had many tremendous staff, plus a team of governors who were determined to renew the school and take the lifeline offered. However, there was a lack of capacity across the staff team and confidence from parents and the community was at an all-time low. The new Year 7 intake numbered 86 children. There were meant to be 235. There was clearly a lot to do.

With the old building up for demolition, we decided to destroy some of our old practices too. Only our best approaches made the move with us, to be joined by some new mission and vision statements, which – looking back – tell a story in themselves:

- Allow teachers to teach.
- Keep learning going.
- Know our children well.

This last one – the need every school must address if it is to take the whole community on its journey – became the mantra for our relationship-led approach to school improvement and provided the platform for our commitment to inclusion.

We quickly witnessed significant improvements built on clear organisational structures – 'controlling the controllables' – and through our tightening up of systems and processes with highly reliable operational procedures.

From the outset, we had a determination to be inclusive – 'every child, every chance' as we called it. What this meant in practice was that we promised that we would *never* permanently exclude a child from the school, while – at the same time – worked to reduce fixed-term exclusions. We also committed to improving progress for *all* pupils through an equity approach that went across every aspect of our curriculum.

Of course, how to remain inclusive and build a brand new culture with the limited resources available was always going to be a challenge. We introduced a range of strategies to build trust and loyalty across the school, working with staff and pupils in order to create capacity for inclusion. Some of these approaches worked and are still working over a decade and a half later. Some fell away once they had served their purpose. The coaching programme was introduced in 2006 and has since become the essential platform for our relationship-led community.

By 2010 we found ourselves in a position where we could revisit and adapt our mission and value statements. To 'Know our children well' we also added:

- Partners in learning.
- Character for learning.
- Enjoy and achieve.

However, what we didn't have was a unified language to help make clear the expectations and the desired impact of this approach. That next leap came to me as a result of working in the Leeds Children's Services team for a period in 2009/10, when I was able to collaborate with Nigel Richardson and colleagues, who were discussing and developing restorative approaches as part of a strategy to change practice and move the directorate out of intervention.

On return to school I was determined to look at whether this approach could provide the structure to support the inclusive approach we had been nurturing for the previous five years. However, the school was used to a way of working that we felt was successful. I was concerned that adopting a restorative approach now would lead to too much change and a weakening of the grip the leaders had on the school. However, too many children were not making the progress they were capable of, we were excluding too many for fixed periods, had too many educated in alternative provision and we were still dependent on having an inclusion/isolation room.

I knew the next step was going to be critical.

To test whether the school was ready for a more restorative approach, I invited Mark Finnis and his team of trainers to introduce the staff to restorative practices, the theory behind it and some of its potential impacts. I was confident that the staff were already working with an inclusive and relationship-led mindset, but I was also aware that the shift to using restorative language and ways of working might be a stretch for us all. The day went well. Mark and his team pitched the training at just the right level for the staff and we never looked back.

One thing became clear right from the outset – a restorative approach is not just about how we resolve conflict when it arises but about how we think, how we make strategy, how the adults behave and what we expect from the children. It quickly became obvious that implementing a restorative approach to leadership and management was not a risk to what we had achieved but actually made us all the more effective, not only in terms of outcomes but also in building capacity and establishing shared ownership and a sense of community across the school. A relational approach substantially supported the school's well-established mission, and values, and had immediate impact on the capacity of the school to move forward.

We set about creating a training programme for all staff – and *all* children – that is continuous and ongoing. We looked to develop and embed a school culture of relationship-led working using restorative practices. Simplicity of language is critical when it comes to helping the school community get, and stay, on board. For us, the three key restorative practices that we find work and are easy to adopt and understand are:

- Engage, explain, expect.
- Build, maintain, repair.
- High challenge and high support.

We embed these in *every* aspect of school – with governors, staff *and* students – and also in our work with parents, partners and other stakeholders.

We continued to work with Mark, Paul Carlile, Paul Moran and others to further develop restorative leadership, intent on making restorative approaches a 'way of being', rather than a set of policies and procedures to follow. We still keep it simple; we do not deviate from our chosen approach and we do not make excuses for non-restorative practice.

Our story is, of course, unique and the 'ducks lined up' for us in a particular way. However, as the leader of the school for 16 years – at the time of writing – I am very clear that the introduction of restorative practice and the springboard of Mark Finnis' training has been the most important strategic decision we have ever made. The domino effect on the way we work and the impact on outcomes has been remarkable. The school has grown into an all-through-school, with nearly 1,500 pupils, up from a roll of just 638. We have a waiting list for each year group and, most importantly, student outcomes and pathways are routinely secure. We have *never* permanently excluded a child. We have had fewer than eight children sent home for a fixed-term exclusion in each of the last four years. We don't have any children in alternative provision. And, I am delighted to say, we shuttered our inclusion/isolation room three years ago.

While our school may be unique, our story is simple, really. Make sure the leaders and staff are committed to going 'the long way round' when necessary. Make sure they are relentless in building and maintaining a culture that promotes the best outcomes for *all* children. Make sure they are all facing in the same direction day after day. Relationships lead to connection and connection leads to community. A community facing in the same direction is a powerful force for change and impact.

We are grateful to Mark for being there at the start of our restorative journey, for advising then and since and, most importantly, for encouraging us to keep developing our practice and understanding. Mark is a national advocate for relational and restorative practices in schools and across all organisations. His work has touched many professionals and impacted on their practice and thereby on the outcomes for so many children and adults. I can wholeheartedly recommend Mark's words of wisdom to you – they will in themselves provide high challenge and high support.

SIMON FLOWERS
EXECUTIVE PRINCIPAL
CARR MANOR COMMUNITY SCHOOL

ACKNOWLEDGEMENTS

This book would not have been possible without the love and support of my wife, Kelly. Thanks from the bottom of my heart for supporting me with your words of encouragement, letting me disappear to work on my book, always making me smile and believing I could get it finished (even when I didn't).

I'd like to acknowledge my wonderful family as a whole and the lads I'm still friends with from school (the Box of Toys) for showing me the way when it comes to the importance of relationships.

To Paul Moran – who is my partner in crime, my sidekick in all things restorative practice since the beginning, and a man I'm proud to call a friend – thanks for your inspiration, support and the fun and smiles along the way.

I'd like to thank my colleagues and friends from my time working in Hull and Leeds. You have influenced my thinking more than you'll ever realise: Nigel Richardson, Estelle McDonald, Paul Carlile, Paul Nixon, Chris Straker, Joanne Faulkner, Michael Vandenbogaerde, Elisabeth Vandenbogaerde, Andy Couldrick, Sharon Inglis, Jennifer Llewellyn, Saleem Tariq, Simon Flowers, Paul Sivak and Gale Burford – thank you.

To my colleagues and friends at L30 Relational Systems, you inspire me each and every day and I'm proud to call you my friends and team.

My own learning wouldn't have been possible without the schools and organisations – large and small – that allowed me to develop my thinking and learning over the last 20 plus years. I'll be forever grateful.

Finally, I'd like to say a sincere thank you to Ian Gilbert, as writing this book has been an exercise in sustained suffering for us both! You have been both supportive and challenging in equal measure. Your unwavering patience, and encouragement, was always delivered in a way that made me smile. Thank you for being my book midwife, for sharpening the glitter pen and for being you.

2021 must be our year of hope.

CONTENTS

Foreword .... *i*

Acknowledgements .... *vii*

First Thoughts 1

    What is this book about? 2

    Why restorative practice? 6

    Restorative practice or restorative justice –
    they're the same thing, aren't they? 9

    Turning the system 12

Chapter 1: Developing a Restorative Mindset **15**

    All behaviour is nothing more than an unmet
    need – the story of David 15

    Connect before content 17

    If you're not modelling what you're teaching,
    you're teaching something different 20

    The 1% principle 21

    Empathy vs sympathy 22

    Make regular deposits into the 'social capital'
    bank 24

    Strike when the iron's cold 27

Chapter 2: Culture, Community and Relationships ... **29**

    Culture exists in every organisation, but is yours
    by design or by default? 29

    Create a sense of belonging 32

    You can't put students first if you put teachers
    last 34

    Know your children (and their families) well and
    allow them to know you well too 36

    Every child (and adult) needs a champion 38

    Build goodwill at good times 40

    Working together works 43

    Significant and important others 44

    Ubuntu and restorative communities 46

Chapter 3: Restorative Conversations and Language .. 49

    Behaviour policy or relationship policy 49

    The power of 'with' 51

    Don't be afraid of the 'L word' 62

    Labels belong on jars 66

    The restorative chat 69

    More questions and fewer answers 70

    Difficult conversations, do they have to be? 71

    Build bridges, not brick walls 76

    The restorative five 78

    The three bubbles 79

    An example from practice 86

    It's not a script, it's just a structure 88

Chapter 4: Restorative Circles 93

    Everything looks better when you put it in a circle ... 93

    Solution-focused circles 96

    The Carr Manor way (part I) 99

    Check-in and check-out circles 100

    Communicating in circles 103

    Preparing for circles to succeed 105

Chapter 5: Restorative Meetings and Conferences 109

    Setting meetings up to succeed 109

    Setting up the seats 112

Running a more formal restorative conference 114

A five-step process for facilitating a restorative conference 118

Conflict as property 121

Chapter 6: Practice Sustainability **125**

One size doesn't fit all; in fact, it only ever fits one .. 125

Planting the seeds of change 127

Making change stick 129

The Carr Manor way (part II) 130

Why change efforts fail 133

Relational leadership 135

Restorative team and department meetings 137

Guiding team 140

Practice development groups 141

Who are the champions? 143

Training students 144

Final Thoughts 147

A list of things to remember – some small and some a bit bigger 147

References and Further Reading *151*

FIRST THOUGHTS

In a school setting, when a student feels more connected to the adults, to their peers and to the school as a whole, they will feel happier and therefore be more productive. We could even think about the 'L word' in this instance. They might love being at school, they might love being with their teachers – or at least certain ones – they might love learning, they might love themselves. After all, it is said often enough that the quality of a student's learning can't exceed the quality of their teachers. But I suggest that neither the quality of the teaching nor of the learning can exceed the quality of the relationship between the teacher and the learner.

I'm sure that few teachers would disagree that the relationships they have with their students matter, but I know that many feel they don't have the time to invest in them thanks to the stresses of our results-focused system, our crowded classrooms and our overcrowded curriculum. What's more, relationships are both simple and hard in equal measure, so it's easy to direct our focus onto the more tangible areas of school life – such as results – and, in doing so, fall into the trap of forgetting that not everything we count counts, and that not everything that counts can be counted.

Do we hit the target but miss the point?

INDEPENDENT THINKING ON RESTORATIVE PRACTICE

WHAT IS THIS BOOK ABOUT?

This, then, is first and foremost a book about relationships.

> The first tool to rethinking success is to review the value of relationships.
>
> **PAOLO GALLO**[1]

A relationship-based school – a relational school, as the terminology goes – puts creating and strengthening the ties of human connection as its number one goal, something that is written through its policies and actions, like the word 'Morecambe' in a stick of rock.

This is a book about compassion.

Empathy can be described as compassion with imagination. Who would turn a blind eye to human suffering when it is right in front of us? What if we were to step outside of ourselves to imagine the suffering of others and then react? Most of the time, there is a reason for a behaviour. Maybe we are part of the problem and, once we understand that, it makes it a lot easier for us to be part of the solution. After all, crime and punishment is easy. Crime and compassion is a lot harder.

This is a book about behaviour.

Despite pressures to the contrary, a relational school does not intentionally shame children. It doesn't dole out punishments like rice at a vegetarian's wedding. It doesn't isolate children, because it remembers that their basic

---

1 P. Gallo, Why Positive Relationships at Work Matter More Than You Think, *World Economic Forum* (16 March 2016). Available at: https://wwwweforum.org/agenda/2016/03/why-positive-relationships-are-key-to-real-success-at-work/.

need is to be connected. Perhaps the behaviour that provokes the punishment of isolation is a misjudged attempt to connect?

This is a book about behaviours.

What if schools were committed to adopting behaviours that promoted consistency in building and managing all relationships? What if they insisted on behaviours that articulated explicitly that creating and strengthening human relationships was the basis of their practice? Everyone involved would be required to challenge and support each other using relational practice as a point of reference. There would need to be agreed processes to follow which strengthen relationships and seek to repair harm when those relationships break down.

This is a book about change.

This book is about how we might adapt, change slightly or even change radically the system and the behaviours that operate within it, to better meet the needs of everyone involved. To say you believe in relationships is simply not enough. We have to be prepared to let go of certainty, of being in control, of always being right, of asserting ourselves because of our age, position or the length of time we've had a staffroom pigeonhole with our name on it. We have to give more time to considering options, to being open rather than closed, to seeking change for the better.

Changing attitudes is at the heart of any change process; this is just as important as changing behaviours. Your attitude grows out of your mental map, the way in which you see the world without needing to look at it, the things you think without actively thinking. Your attitude is what lies behind your behaviours. Change your attitude and watch the dominoes fall.

This is a book about children and young people.

> ... in order to develop normally, a child requires progressively more complex joint activity with one or more adults who have an irrational emotional relationship with the child. Somebody's got to be crazy about that kid. That's number one. First, last, and always.
>
> **URIE BRONFENBRENNER**[2]

This is a book about leadership, whatever your role.

Change *from* is one thing. Change *to* is where leadership comes in. 'What will it look like when it's done?' as the saying goes. We need, therefore, a shared vision *and* a strategy for building that vision. An organisation with relationships truly at the centre, and a vision owned by everyone and understood by all. The vision needs to be clearly communicated and backed up with strong leadership, leadership that exists at all levels and across all areas, driven by those who command respect for their personal attributes rather than their status.

This, in turn, requires clear priorities for the entire staff community, with key actions and objectives owned by everyone. To grow this requires not only specialist and bespoke training, but also the development of local thinking – what does that look like here, in our context, with these children, in this community, at this time?

This is a book about communities.

---

2 Quoted in National Scientific Council on the Developing Child, *Young Children Develop in an Environment of Relationships*. Working Paper No. 1 (Cambridge, MA: Harvard University Center on the Developing Child, 2004), p. 1. Available at: https://developingchild.harvard.edu/wp-content/uploads/2004/04/Young-Children-Develop-in-an-Environment-of-Relationships.pdf.

The restorative world that I am describing shares 'power' across communities and with families. It acknowledges people and communities as experts in their own solutions. It utilises informal restorative meetings in everyday situations, and more formal restorative conferences when there are serious concerns to be addressed. It uses proactive and/or responsive approaches to address concerns safely, empower change and maximise personal responsibility.

This is a book about collaboration.

At a time of shortage, resources need to be focused on responses to unwanted behaviour and conflict that are efficient, effective and, more importantly, which meet the needs of the school community and wider society. It must be a multi-agency, cross-service approach, involving criminal justice, education, social care, housing, police, healthcare providers, the voluntary sector and all other key partners – working together so that children and families experience coherence.

This is a book about restorative practice.

Put all these things together and you have a vision of restorative practice. Do them all and you have restorative practice in action. I am proposing, then, that restorative practice is the central delivery concept in everything a community does. It is the glue that binds together all services, with common values owned by all, and builds the bridge between teachers and children, and schools and communities.

This book is an introduction to restorative practice, not a how-to guide. I will share what it is and, in so doing, together we can understand better what it isn't. For example, we start with the distinction between restorative justice and restorative practice, as confusing the two is like referring to the Scottish as 'English'.

Just remember while you read, there is, as we at Independent Thinking keep banging on about, always another way.

WHY RESTORATIVE PRACTICE?

Every day, in lots of different ways, our students ask: do I matter to you, do you notice me, do I belong here? And, if we aren't careful – because actions speak louder than words – the answer will be seen in the behaviours that play out. It's not always what we say or what we do, but how we do it and how students end up feeling.

I've been working with children, young people, families and across communities for over 20 years now and in a range of settings. In the early part of my career I often thought that it was my job to have all the answers. As the person in a position of authority, that it was up to me to find the answers rather than ask the right questions to help others find their answers. That it fell to me to dole out solutions, to rescue children or to make excuses for their behaviour, or, often, that of the adults. I guess you can easily get sucked into that way of working when you spend long enough in organisations in which that's how the system operates. You learn to silence that voice in your head shouting, 'Just because we've always done it that way, it doesn't mean it's not incredibly stupid!'

Of course, it's difficult to change, to move away from traditions, especially in areas of society in which traditions are held up as a good thing, such as education. It's like folding your arms the other way, or putting the other sock on first, or supporting Liverpool; it's just wrong. Within seconds of folding your arms the 'wrong' way, you will have refolded them the 'right' way. It's hard to break habits and because it's hard, and because humans don't tend to like hard, we go for the easy route and think we can get away with it by calling it 'tradition'.

Yet doing things better means doing things differently, which, in turn, means that we need to be ready for those feelings of discomfort: up for embracing them rather than avoiding them. We need to start striving to be better at discovering how we can stop doing old things and start doing new ones. Or, at the very least, to do old things in new ways. After all, the most dangerous phrase in any organisation is: 'We've always done it that way around here.' Not because the old way was wrong by definition, but because you aren't questioning whether it might be.

Now, don't get me wrong, lots of practices, policies and systems *do* work, but do they work for everyone, all of the time? How inclusive are they? Do they serve to create and strengthen connections across the organisation? After all, for the organisation to flourish, that's got to be the measure. Or, as I tell schools when delivering restorative practice training, 'connect before content' (see Chapter 1 for more on this, especially in our post-COVID world). After all, as humans, we are hardwired to want to connect and to belong. It's how we've lasted so long as a species.

Schools that explicitly put a greater focus on proactively building and maintaining relationships will find that there will be fewer occasions when relationships break down and, therefore, there is a need for them to be repaired. Getting involved earlier in the life of a problem will also help. For children to feel able to talk, you need adults who are willing to listen. When we have adults who are unwilling to listen, we end up with children who are unwilling to talk.

The ultimate goal is the adoption of restorative principles to inspire communities to feel able to shape their own futures. This is aimed at providing them with the confidence to resolve their own problems and generate their own values. Children, families and professionals all need to spend time investing in their own social capital, being proactive in capitalising on relationships and putting the repair of harm and relationship breakdowns as a key priority. We want to encourage a shift away from a reactionary culture, in which our responses are often emotional and un-thought-through, to a more considered and responsible approach.

Such an undertaking needs everyone to act explicitly, across the whole school, with these goals in mind. This entails keeping a close eye on our own behaviours and habitual practices – which speak louder than any list of values on a lanyard, poster or school website – and ensure that we treat everyone with respect. We must involve people in decisions that affect them, listen actively to each other, be empathic and deal with conflicts and tensions in a way that seeks to repair harm and sustain relationships. This is the core of restorative practice.

FIRST THOUGHTS

RESTORATIVE PRACTICE OR RESTORATIVE JUSTICE – THEY'RE THE SAME THING, AREN'T THEY?

Restorative practice and restorative justice are often confused as being the same thing. They're not – not quite. Don't get me wrong, they both come under the same umbrella, with similar values, beliefs, skills and practices.

Both do *with* rather than *to* or *for*.

Both are all about relationships.

Both are about culture.

Both have clear principles of treating students justly and those principles drive our practice.

Both restorative justice and practice give us a very clear framework to hang our practice on.

Both are about relationships – one more building and one more repairing.

Both support students to recognise that all of their actions affect others.

Both help students to consider how best to prevent harm and manage conflict.

Both create contexts that restore.

Both are transformational.

One comes a little earlier and one comes a little later.

Both are common sense, but, sadly, common sense isn't always that common. So, let's make common sense common practice.

Restorative justice is an approach specifically used when resolving conflict and repairing harm. It enables those who have been hurt to come together with those who caused the hurt to explore and acknowledge the impact of their actions and take the necessary steps to put things right.

Restorative practice describes a way of being, an underpinning ethos, which enables us to build and maintain healthy relationships. It provides a strong framework within which we can promote a whole-school ethos founded on the importance of relationships. This includes a range of approaches to managing conflict and tensions in a way that repairs harm and mends relationships if and when those relationships do break down.

Before a school can deal with conflict and tensions effectively it must first build up the relationships. This will then allow those affected to be able to come back together. A teacher I worked alongside in a school in Hull once said to me, 'How can we seek to rebuild relationships with some of our students, if there is no relationship there in the first place?' George had a point.

In this way, schools seek to find inclusive and effective approaches that manage and ultimately aim to transform a range of behaviours – exhibited by adults as well as by children and young people. Learning Together is one example of a whole-school restorative practice programme for secondary schools. It comprises training for staff in restorative practice as well as a school action group involving staff and students which oversees implementation and ensures school policies and systems are supportive. An evaluation using a randomised controlled trial found lower rates of bullying in programme schools versus comparison schools after three years.[3] Students in programme schools also reported lower rates of smoking, drinking and drug use and higher rates of mental well-being and quality of life. The intervention was rated as highly cost effective. Evidence seems to show that such approaches positively impact on attendance and attainment, reduces exclusions, and improves mental and emotional health, parent/career engagement, staff retention and the wider transformation of the school culture.[4]

Restorative practice also focuses on a systemic and, importantly, relational shift that is much needed to create a secure and safe environment to improve the emotional well-being of all. It also includes working with families to find shared solutions around their child's education, behaviour and well-being, ensuring that they are safeguarded and protected but also empowered and responsible.

Restorative practice is not about replacing traditional behaviour management systems. It's certainly not about

---

[3] C. Bonell et al., Effects of the Learning Together Intervention on Bullying and Aggression in English Secondary Schools (INCLUSIVE): A Cluster Randomised Controlled Trial, *Lancet* 392 (2018): 2452-2464.

[4] For example, a Department for Education review noted the positive impact of restorative approaches on bullying. F. Thompson and P. K. Smith, *The Use and Effectiveness of Anti-Bullying Strategies in Schools*. Research Report DFE-RR098 (London: Department for Education, 2011). In the USA, positive outcomes have been found by researchers, see, for example: C. H. Augustine, J. Engberg, G. E. Grimm, E. Lee, E. Lin Wang, K. Christianson and A. A. Joseph, *Can Restorative Practices Improve School Climate and Curb Suspensions? An Evaluation of the Impact of Restorative Practices in a Mid-Sized Urban School District* (Santa Monica, CA: RAND Corporation, 2018). Available at: https://www.rand.org/pubs/research_reports/RR2840.html. For more on attendance and exclusions, see: L. Skinns, N. Du Rose and M. Hough, *An Evaluation of Bristol RAiS* (London: Institute for Criminal Policy Research and King's College London, 2009). Available at: https://restorativejustice.org.uk/sites/default/files/resources/files/Bristol%20RAiS%20full%20report.pdf.

being soft or turning a blind eye to poor behaviour, no matter what the *Daily Mail* or strident voices on Twitter might say. It's about elevating the culture of a school or organisation so people are pulled in, not pushed out, about fostering a greater sense of community and a communal ownership of control and fear, about encouraging a willingness to act in the right way for the right reasons. In this way, a restorative school is so much harder to create than a culture of compliance. Compliance is easy, encouraging as it does an abnegation of responsibility by both parties. 'Follow the rules or I'll kick you out' is easy to say. 'Fine, I don't want to do what you say, so I'll be kicked out' is easy to do. But here we miss an opportunity to create something better.

Although its roots are clearly in restorative justice – as a way of repairing the harm done to the community and relationships within it – restorative practice has the bolder ambition of proactively developing the sense of community and seeking to increase the social capital between people and across the school and, from there, into the wider community.

Put simply, restorative justice is what you do; restorative practice is what you are.

TURNING THE SYSTEM

We're right at the crux of all matters restorative now, so let's unpick things a little more by looking at the system of retribution that so many schools have in place and the way in which it ends up causing more harm than the original transgression. How many behaviour management systems are currently set up in the following way?

- The 'what happened?' part is all about gathering facts as quickly as possible.
- Next, we turn to finding out, equally quickly, who is to blame.
- We then identify which rule has been broken.
- Then we work out what an appropriate punishment might be, one that fits the crime. Here we can be creative (you dropped litter so you will spend all lunchtime picking up litter) or, given how busy we are, just slot the student into the nearest passing discipline event or process (whole-school detentions on Wednesday; curriculum-area detentions on Thursday; we have a vacancy in isolation booth 3 a week on Friday, see you there …).
- We get on with our lives thinking that something has changed, lessons have been learned and we're all bigger and better because of it.
- Repeat.

Apart from the damage done to the relationship between the transgressor and the authority, the students and colleagues who were harmed have been ignored and accountability for any sense of closure is placed squarely at the door of the punishment. Justice has prevailed, so let's move on.

A restorative view, however, seeks to create a better sort of system, one which sets about things slightly differently:

- The 'what happened?' element is designed to give everyone involved an opportunity to share their unique perspectives (remember, at any time there is always my truth, your truth and *the* truth).
- Next, we ask who has been affected and how.

- This is followed by examining and exploring the impact on people and relationships.
- We draw things together by asking the 'needs' questions – what needs are there and what needs to happen to repair damage and allow us to move forward?

This alternative structure of thought and practice moves us towards a much more interpersonal process: a culture of shared responsibility and problem solving. The voices and needs of all those involved are clearly outlined and addressed, and – while some sort of punishment may well be necessary – the focus is on restoring trust and connection, on putting things right, making things better and moving forward.

Let's begin by looking in more detail at how we can shift our mindsets, as that, in turn, will begin to shape our actions.

CHAPTER 1
DEVELOPING A RESTORATIVE MINDSET

ALL BEHAVIOUR IS NOTHING MORE THAN AN UNMET NEED – THE STORY OF DAVID

David arrived at school 15 minutes late and wearing white trainers. He was greeted with a pointy finger to the chest.

'Why are you late and where are your black shoes?'

'F@*$ off,' was the response.

David was sent to his head of year and along the way told three more people to do the same.

David was excluded that day.

Let me tell you about David (this is a lesson in knowing your students well).

He is 11 years old and lives with his mum and his younger brother and sister.

The reason he arrived late to school was because he was dropping his brother and sister off at primary school. Those white trainers, he isn't wearing them to look cool. It's the only footwear he has and, if you look closely, you'll see that they are in pretty poor condition. In fact, he is embarrassed by them.

If you knew David well, you'd know that David's house hasn't got carpet on the floor in any of the rooms, not that there are that many. David hasn't got his own bedroom; in fact, he hasn't even got his own bed. He has a mattress on the kitchen floor.

If you knew David well, you'd know David is on a child protection plan, and maybe you'd question how good an idea it is to send him home for three days. If you knew David well, you'd know that we need him in school to know he is safe while we work closely with other agencies and, more importantly, his family.

He is on free school meals and we're not sure he gets regular meals when he isn't at school. Maybe he does (I was on free school meals at school and did get fed well at home), but we don't know that for sure.

David doesn't go to sleep until his mum does as only then does he know his mum is safe. This is because there is domestic violence and abuse in David's house.

But then you'd know all this, if you knew David well.

There is a phrase that has been around in our work with children and families for a long time and it's 'all behaviour is nothing more than a display of unmet needs'. If that is the case – and there are many who choose to disagree – then the simplest way to change the behaviour is to address the child's unmet needs. Or, to put it another way, children who are loved at home come into school to learn; those who aren't loved at home come into school to be loved.

You will have had a David in your school. Knowing what you know now, how would you react to his behaviour – his unmet need – differently? The desire to jab your finger at his chest and overreact at his reaction may still be strong but, remember, relational approaches are what count.

Such a response will do damage, both now and in the longer term. A knee-jerk act is not in your interests and is certainly not in David's. So, what do you do?

What would I do? Well, of course, I would have corrected the issue over school uniform. Rules are rules after all. But note the verb. Correcting is different from correction.

But first, above everything else, I would have greeted David that morning with the biggest smile I could give him and told him how pleased I was to see him. I would have asked if he had had breakfast, placed a hand on his shoulder, shaken his hand, looked into his eyes and said, 'I'm here for you.'

You have no idea what students are dealing with in their own life. So just be nice – it's that simple.

CONNECT BEFORE CONTENT

> Without relatedness, no work can occur. […] Connect before content.
>
> **PETER BLOCK**[1]

Never underestimate the power of this simple premise. Do you connect with students, their families and colleagues at the outset, before you go anywhere near the content? If so, how?

If we aren't careful, we put our focus on the content and forget to simply connect. Our students need connection

---

1 P. Block, *Community: The Structure of Belonging* (San Francisco, CA: Berrett-Koehler Publishers, 2008), p. 98, p. 146.

as well as the important content. The connection creates the space to then be able to explore the content. Connections can happen by themselves, but wouldn't you want them to happen intentionally?

Meaningful learning takes place when we have meaningful relationships. What we are seeking to do is to positively affect the mindset of our students as they come into lessons, our visitors as they come into school and our colleagues as they come into meetings. We do this through the look on our faces, the way we greet each other, our tone of voice and our body language, as much as through things we actually say. It's about how we talk among ourselves, how we act among ourselves, how we are there for each other. It's about the weather we create around us.

Remember the old joke about the pub on the moon that shut down because there was no atmosphere? How does your classroom compare? If your office was a coffee shop, would you be a regular? Having people leave your presence feeling better than when they arrived is one thing, but what about helping people feel better just by coming through the door?

The start of the day as students arrive can often be the busiest and most unsettled part of the school day. Getting involved earlier in the life of any problems can often help you have fewer problems later. Be more proactive and less reactive. I often think that when I'm reactive, it's emotional and not thought through; when I'm responsive, it's regulated and thought through. If I'm not regulated with my own emotions, I'll never be able to help regulate a student's.

Greeting students at the school gate with a smile (remember, smiling at students is good for you both), a 'good morning', or a 'How are you?', will give you a quick temperature check to see how their day might work out. Most of all, it's important that we start the day on a positive note. Waiting for students at the classroom door gives us another opportunity to connect, saying their name correctly – that's the subtle difference – and remembering things about them. Not only do smiles make us feel good, they have the tendency of getting passed on to others. A simple positive greeting can have an impact on all the things we want to improve: learning, behaviour and, most of all, belonging.

There are many examples in schools around the world of handshakes, hugs and high fives at the classroom door (and post-COVID these will become more elaborate and creative I'm sure). Some colleagues even develop complex, personalised handshakes that are unique to each child. These are all utterly brilliant examples of connecting before tackling the content and show how simple acts like this can create a different culture and different behaviours from the off.

In our post-COVID world, maybe you are more wary of human contact than you were before. How about a smile, a 'nice one', a 'good morning', an 'it's great to see you', a 'have a great day', an 'enjoy your next lesson' and, at the end of the day, a simple 'goodbye, have a great evening, see you in the morning'. Who knows, they may even reciprocate!

Of course, such positivity and high fivery might not suit everyone all of the time. If we really know our students well, we know the ones who will need to be greeted in a different way. For students for whom this type of welcome might create disconnection, allow them to develop their own way of arriving into the classroom. This is important for you as the teacher too. Your needs are also important, don't forget. That said, there are few people for whom a smile, even if it is not returned, does not go a long, long way.

Your success in creating a positive and productive school depends more than anything else on the quality of the relationships within it, especially those that the adults build with the children. When students feel liked, respected and trusted by their teachers, they find more success in school, academically and behaviourally. Those staff–student relationships influence everything and, while this might sound obvious, it's obvious when you visit schools in which this is not the priority. You can see it in the time they spend on behavioural issues, chasing achievements rather than celebrating them.

IF YOU'RE NOT MODELLING WHAT YOU'RE TEACHING, YOU'RE TEACHING SOMETHING DIFFERENT

Modelling is like breathing. You can't not do it. You are modelling behaviour for your students, whether you mean to or not. So, if you're not modelling what you're teaching, then you're not really teaching what you think you're teaching. Students see whether you're showing warmth and respect towards them and to the other students and adults in your school. Often, they will model their own behaviour after your behaviour, albeit subconsciously.

Take, for example, the manner in which you manage your emotions. Students notice the methods you use to manage how you're feeling. They notice the positive strategies you employ, such as taking a deep breath or talking about your frustrations. Likewise, they notice your negative strategies, such as shouting or making disrespectful jokes about colleagues. Be aware that students will often copy the strategies you use, just like they might emulate parents' or carers' behaviours.

So, the behaviours you want? You've got to give them to get them.

THE 1% PRINCIPLE

Through reading about the great success of the British Cycling team and the inspiring work of Sir Dave Brailsford around marginal gains and the 1% principle,[2] it really got me thinking connecting this to my work around relationships. Small ripples create big waves and that's where the 1% principle comes in. The small stuff often becomes the big stuff. It can be frustrating when we focus on big changes as they can become overwhelming, they don't get done or we wonder how we'll find the time. Small acts quickly mount up, and that's where we get continuous improvements. 1% at a time can work brilliantly.

How do you eat an elephant? One bite at a time.

What are the small wins that you could find, the tweaks to a policy or process you currently do? What minor thing could you do differently as you walk to your classroom? When you phone a parent or carer, a 1% marginal gain might be the difference between getting a polite response and genuinely getting them on side. Compare 'Good morning, class' with 'Good morning! It's nice to see you all

---

2 M. Slater, Olympics Cycling: Marginal Gains Underpin Team GB Dominance, *BBC Sport* (8 August 2012). Available at: https://www.bbc.co.uk/sport/olympics/19174302.

and I'm so excited to be sharing X, Y and Z with you today.' Add a smile and that's another 1%.

I have a friend who runs marathons and when I ask how he does it, he says one mile at a time. This idea runs contrary to the premise that for big results, you need big changes. Instead, it suggests that big results are the result of little changes, lots of them. It's the same when we look at building better relationships in our schools. If you want to improve relationships across the school, focus on the many mini daily relational actions. In other words, don't worry about doing the principles of restorative practice 100% better. Just do 100 restorative things 1% better.

EMPATHY VS SYMPATHY

Empathy is a great way of building connection. Sharing with students how you *feel* – and exploring how they feel – can open up really useful conversations about how everyone can work together better. Contrary to popular belief, teachers aren't kept in the store cupboard overnight; they aren't machines (not yet anyway). They are, in fact, humans with human feelings.

It's easy to leave our human side at home and see sharing those feelings as a sign of weakness, but a teacher's human side can be used as a way to build compassion and connection with students and across school communities. Real reconciliation in relationships can occur when we are able to talk about what happened, what bothered us, how we felt about it and how we could avoid hurting each other in the future.

Can we come off as weak if we share how we feel and reveal a level of vulnerability to our students, I hear you ask? After all, weakness is often the last thing we are willing to show at school. 'Don't smile till Christmas', you can still remember the teacher-trainers telling you. 'Never show any sign of weakness,' they said, 'they can smell fear.'

Now, don't get me wrong. It does take courage to show weakness. Saying, 'I need help' or 'I own that mistake' or 'When you said that, I felt this or that emotion' takes guts. But openness breeds openness in a relational school. In order to inspire students to walk this path, we have to go there first. We cannot pretend that human feelings are something that only happens to others. We have to experience feelings *with* our students, which requires both an acknowledgement that our own feelings exist and a desire to understand theirs. In creating the right space for this conversation, we also create and strengthen the connections with our students.

One strategy is to begin by naming the behaviour that is bothering you, telling them the feeling you experience as a result of it and checking in with them to see how it makes them feel. After all, how we feel is how we feel, even if it's just at that moment and it's not actually reality. Feelings can be facts to that student at that moment and that's something you can connect around. You can argue about whose perspective is right regarding a behaviour or action, but feelings are feelings. What impact are we having on each other at a human level and are we happy with it?

What we are doing here is modelling and exploring the concept of empathy, a critical skill in any successful relationship and part of the fabric of a school practising in a restorative way. According to the foremost expert in such matters, Brené Brown, there are four important steps to take when it comes to showing empathy:

1 *Perspective taking, or putting yourself in someone else's shoes.*

2 *Staying out of judgement and listening.*

3 *Recognising emotion in another person that you have maybe felt before.*

4 *Communicating that you can recognise that emotion.*[3]

And as for the difference between empathy and its less-welcome cousin sympathy, again, Brené Brown sums it up succinctly:

Empathy fuels connection. Sympathy drives disconnection.[4]

MAKE REGULAR DEPOSITS INTO THE 'SOCIAL CAPITAL' BANK

There is a great deal of talk currently about cultural and social capital and the need for young people to be developing it through their time in school. Social capital involves the networks children can tap into as they mature, assets developed through establishing and maintaining positive, healthy relationships with peers and others, whereas cultural capital is the acquisition of a particular type of culturally desirable knowledge, which means you can operate with fluency within social groups, particularly upper- and middle-class ones. Capital in any form is a resource you can call on when you need it. But before you

---

3 RSA, Brené Brown on Empathy [video] (10 December 2013). Available at: https://wwwyoutube.com/watch?v=1Evwgu369Jw.

4 RSA, Brené Brown on Empathy.

can do that, you need to acquire it. This is where teachers come in.

Imagine a glass jar held by every student. This is the piggy bank in which they keep their social capital. This jar is where they deposit the social capital that you – and others – are giving them. And not just one or two deposits. Loads. Some children might be coming into school with that jar already overflowing. They are the lucky ones. Others might come into school without anything in their relationship bank at all. They may even be in debt. These are the children who are going to need those social deposits more than the others, more than anything. A smile as they come through the door? Ker-ching – that's a deposit. How's your little brother settling in at school? Ker-ching – there's another. Did you watch the match last night? What a shower United have become these days – jackpot! The deposits keep rolling in and what's it taken? Seconds? Minutes at the most?

Is it easier or harder to challenge a student when you have that relational capital? Have you ever noticed those teachers or pastoral staff who can just give a child a quiet look and they will take their coat off, put away their mobile phone and take their seat, when others battle to get the same student to comply? These professionals know that, if they have topped the relationship bank up enough, they can draw on that social capital if and when things go wrong. Even better, if we are topping up all students' relationship banks, we can draw on them individually and collectively, and they can draw on the deposits they make in the adults' relationship banks too. If there is no relationship there in the first place – if that jar is empty or running in debt – when things go wrong there is nothing to draw on: no contingency, no rainy-day fund to see us through the bad times.

The challenge is planning how we can make these deposits with as many students as we can. How do we seek out opportunities for deposits to be made? How do we make those deposits with students who are not in our classes or year group? How do you make deposits across the staff team and not just with those colleagues in our key stage or department? It's all about the deposits we make. But where to start? Here's a good list: pay attention, laugh with them, greet at the classroom door or, better yet, the school gate, end lessons on a good note, learn to apologise, develop and cultivate compassion, high five in the corridor or at the classroom door or offer a smile instead (especially during COVID times) if they don't like the contact, steal a crisp at lunchtime (but not the whole bag), look out for their team's results, teach the child and not the curriculum, show and tell (it's not just for kids), remember their birthday, jump rope with them at playtime, give consistently but receive occasionally, brag about them outrageously to others, tell them what your favourite box set or film is and your first name.

Go on, let's name a few more: remember that each day is new day, be their biggest cheerleader, let go of the past, be authentic, earn their respect and then expect it in return, share a pen or a pencil, say goodbye at the end of the day, never use sarcasm and believe in them.

Remember though, children don't just want us to believe in them, they want to believe that we believe in them.

STRIKE WHEN THE IRON'S COLD

In the moment is sometimes – dare I say, often – the worst time to react to something you're not happy with if your bigger goal is to keep relationships at the heart of all you do. Bringing your emotions to bear on your relationships is important, as we have seen; however, this does not mean that they should be allowed to take charge. The secret is to use them at the right time, to the right degree and in the right place. When emotions are running really high, we would do well to take a moment or two to allow them to settle. Of course, there will be times when this takes more than a moment and it is important to wait for the right time to have whatever restorative conversation is needed to put things right again.

One of the reasons why reacting in the moment makes things worse is that often, especially in a busy school environment, it can make for a very public spectacle. Reprimanding someone in front of an audience is a very different act – and will incite very different reactions and consequences – to saying the same things but in private. The same goes for CC-ing others into your angry email. Making things public introduces a new dynamic into the exchange: it has moved us away from restoration to a position in which winning – or losing – face is what counts.

That reprimand might well be necessary but take it somewhere private and you'll be surprised at the result. That angry email might be necessary too but CC-ing in the wider team probably isn't. That said, my golden rule for angry emails is that writing and sending them are two different things. Often writing one is a very cathartic process and allows you to vent your feelings in a 'better out than in' way. You're allowed to feel angry and hurt and to validate those feelings by putting them into words. The important thing is just *not* to send it. Write it, check it, notice how you feel, possibly share it with a critical friend, and then save it in drafts. The next day, you'll often be amazed at two things. Firstly, how the situation has resolved amicably and professionally in the meantime and, secondly, that you are really pleased you didn't send it as you now realise it would have only made things worse. After all, where did we get the crazy idea that in order to make children – or indeed anyone – do better, we first have to make them feel worse?

Given that all behaviour is telling us something if we choose to open our ears, it is worth remembering that, while some people may well need a good talking to, many actually just need a damn good listening to.

CHAPTER 2
CULTURE, COMMUNITY AND RELATIONSHIPS

CULTURE EXISTS IN EVERY ORGANISATION, BUT IS YOURS BY DESIGN OR BY DEFAULT?

> Culture eats strategy for breakfast.
>
> **OFTEN ATTRIBUTED TO PETER DRUCKER**[1]

The reason why this quote is so popular – even given its unclear origins – is because it is so true. No matter what strategy you have in place, if the culture isn't right, it will never work. After all, people often aren't resisting the changes we are trying to make per se, they are resisting the way in which they are being told to make them.

Put simply, culture is the complex and broad set of relationships, values, attitudes and behaviours that bind a specific community consciously and unconsciously. It is usefully defined as 'The way we do things around here' – something understood and subscribed to by the whole school community.

---

[1] See https://quoteinvestigator.com/2017/05/23/culture-eats/.

So, how do you change the culture of a school? One classroom at a time.

Where do you start? In the one you're in now.

To create something new, you have to come to terms with the current reality and that starts with looking not at what the young people are doing but at how the adults are behaving. After all, if you're not modelling what you're teaching, then you're teaching something different. Modelling matters. And with restorative practice, it's important to model the model.

Let me give you an example from chez Finnis. Last night I was shouting up the stairs for one of my children to come down for tea ('dinner' if you're from Cheshire). Receiving no answer, I gradually started to shout a little louder. Eventually the recalcitrant child came out of his room and I informed him again that his tea was ready. Later that evening, once he had returned to his room, he was shouting at me from upstairs, whereupon I challenged him to come downstairs and have a conversation with me rather than shout. We've all been there. Modelling what we teach … I think not. 'Do what I say and not what I do' is fine if you are a Victorian patriarch, but 'Do what I do' is really how it works.

Once we understand that all of the actions of all of the adults in your school make a contribution to school culture, then we understand that changing the behaviour of our students starts with us. Together as a staff, and collectively with students, we need to be clear about the vision we hold, the behaviours we expect to see from each other and how we build expectations and boundaries that strengthen relationships and build trust.

What can help here is putting together a short list of expected norms, needs, expectations and behaviours – a quick menu of 'How we act around here when the leadership isn't looking.' It needs to be as simple as possible (I told you relationships are simple) – for example, be respectful and kind, take responsibility, and never give up. And with each one, we also build in the expectation that we – everyone in the school, adults included – will always support others to do the same. As with any change process, simplicity is key and less is more. What's important isn't what you put up on the website or display proudly in the entrance to the school, it is the ways in which it lives and breathes in everyday practice.

Furthermore, when the process for developing this list is fair and performed across the whole school as a community, then the community is more likely to go along with it. All parties, including parents and students, need to be engaged in making decisions, so they can come to a shared understanding of what the expectations look like in practice and understand the consequences if they don't stick to what's been agreed. The process, in this way, becomes as important as the outcome.

Whatever school you find yourself in, it will have a culture whether you have specifically articulated what you want it to be or not. Restorative practice is about making the implicit explicit, making the invisible visible. Having an explicit framework gives us something to hang our practice onto so we can then act *on purpose*, deliberately and, from there, creatively. We can also use that framework to hold others responsible for their behaviours. After all, you can't expect children to know how to behave if you've never told them your expectations.

A new culture is not something that is created overnight. It cannot be achieved by planning alone or by rebranding in corporate colours. It is created by sharing a vision, beliefs, values and behaviours that breathe life into the organisation. It cannot be achieved by one person, even if that person started the search for a new culture. It has to be owned and driven by people, and groups of people, and groups of groups of people.

To what extent is your school a restorative, relational environment currently? How far does it have to travel to be as successful as it can be in this new culture? What action is necessary to help it get there? After all, as the saying goes, a goal without a plan is just a wish. But give a wish a plan.

CREATE A SENSE OF BELONGING

> We are a community of possibilities, not a community of problems.
>
> **PETER BLOCK**[2]

The social fabric of a school must be formed from expanding everyone's sense of belonging, their palpable sense of feeling interconnected. This is built on the notion that only when we care for the well-being of the whole school community is true community built. We must engineer a shift to the belief that students have the ability to create a safe school along with us. Achieving this is incredibly complex (I told you relationships were hard) and can only be done by undertaking a strong commitment to *all* members of the school community and creating values, behaviours, systems and policies that work for all.

---

2 Block, *Community*, p. 30.

We need to nurture this strong sense of belonging as we work to strengthen and further connect our school communities. This must happen one meeting at a time, one classroom at a time and one person at a time. After all, small ripples can create big waves. We won't achieve our aims, however, if we have a culture that's built on fear, control and an outmoded authoritarian approach.

What would your school community need to do to transform the culture? In answering this question, don't just think about making things a little better, but *very* different from what you have now. How are you going to be with each other as you achieve it? What conversations will take place as the change happens? What are the possibilities? As you think these questions through, remember to focus on gifts, not deficits, strengths, not weaknesses, and solutions, not problems (and be cautious here as some people have a problem for every solution – you know who they are ...).

Just as human beings have a basic need for food and shelter, we also have a basic need to belong to a group and form relationships. In other words, what *can't* we achieve with a team when they feel that they belong? In simple terms, each student thinks 'I matter around here, and I am noticed. I feel interconnected with those around me: in my class, in my year group and across my school.' What if we didn't sit on different sides of the table, we all sat on the same side? For our young people, when they feel they belong at school, they also feel respected and ready to learn. That's why great teachers work so hard to create a classroom environment in which every student feels able to contribute and be heard – not just the 'good' ones, the 'bright' ones, the ones making their voices heard, the 'ones like me'.

Classroom norms and expectations that put relationships and belonging at the heart of things are vital for making sure that everyone is on the same page about how to treat one another in academic spaces. And when the students have a say in compiling these expectations, they are even more powerful.

YOU CAN'T PUT STUDENTS FIRST IF YOU PUT TEACHERS LAST

It's true what they say, we only learn to care by being shown care. Good teachers will always put children and young people first – and that's how it should be – but good leaders make sure that the school community is one in which *everyone* is cared for. They never lose sight of the fact that before we are teachers, we are human beings. Restorative schools always remember that. They understand that unless teachers feel cared for they might resign their effort even if they do not quit the school.

Learning how to boost teacher morale, increase engagement, provide authentic recognition and build trust between all members of the staff community is a daily task, not something for an INSET day or a national 'thank a teacher' campaign. So, how do we make space to create a culture of appreciation, support and open communication about mental and emotional healthcare? Well, this list offers a few starting points. See what you think:

- Focus on what you can control and not what you can't.

- Check on your classroom neighbours and let them check on you.

- It's always important to do the right thing, whatever the right thing is.
- As they tell you to on a plane, put your own oxygen mask on first.
- Smile. It's good for everyone.
- Give consistently, receive occasionally.
- Staying positive doesn't mean you have to be happy all the time.
- Fear can sometimes be a liar.
- Don't believe everything you think.
- Less is more only when more is too much.
- Be a no-ego doer.
- Work on things that matter the most today.
- Don't think less of yourself, just think of yourself a little less.
- It's all about making common sense common practice.
- Engage in dialogue with others even when it's difficult.
- Eye contact is good, unless you're eating a banana.
- When people don't feel heard they get louder.
- Conflict properly managed is absolutely essential.
- The removal of threat is not the same as creating safety.
- Create systems as well as behaviours that are capable of caring.
- Other people's negativity isn't worth worrying about.

- Everything works somewhere but nothing works everywhere.
- Be careful you don't hit the target but miss the point.
- Relationships aren't built in a day; they are built daily.

Always remember, you are not expected to set yourself on fire to keep other people warm.

KNOW YOUR CHILDREN (AND THEIR FAMILIES) WELL AND ALLOW THEM TO KNOW YOU WELL TOO

We have to give something of ourselves, to connect on a human level, to see each other as people rather than purely as a student or a teacher. Know the child before you know the student; know the person before you know the parent or carer; know the person before you know the colleague; know the person before you know the leader. You get the message. We're humans first and foremost, all of us.

Each and every child – and colleague – is different, and we can only appreciate their uniqueness if we know them well, if we understand their strengths and their weaknesses and find out what makes them tick. Students will be curious and want to know who their teachers are as people. That's why bumping into one shopping for underwear in M&S is always such a big event in their lives.

When I talk with colleagues about this, it often causes heated discussions around what to share. Should we share anything that's of a more personal or even private nature, or keep things strictly professional? Let's be clear, we aren't talking about sharing anything that is or feels uncomfortably private. What I am suggesting is that revealing a little of yourself as a human being is crucial for effective relationship building to occur.

Our professional role is fundamental because it underpins our relationship with the child as a student. Placing the emphasis on our roles and responsibilities, our professional subject knowledge, our understanding of policies, practice and professional standards, is vital. The professional 'us' makes the relationship with the child purposeful, because, as professionals, we will have particular aims for the child – this is true for teachers and for any other professional adults in their lives. The personal self, however, is more about how we engage with the child in a way that shows them who we are, so that we can develop a better, more authentic relationship with them, which, in turn, will feed into our efficacy as professionals.

We also should not confuse personal with private. Everything that is private is personal but not everything that is personal is private. We can share things that happen in our personal lives. What we are doing through knowing our students well and allowing them to know us is modelling the potential that two human beings have for relating to each other with respect and for the benefit of each other.

Of course, when performing the dance between the personal and the professional we must be self-aware, constantly reflecting in the moment and afterwards and being happy to take advice and feedback from others. It is certainly not about making ourselves unduly vulnerable or giving a warts-and-all report on our love lives after a heavy weekend. What it is, is understanding that sharing a little of ourselves can go a long way.

I'll happily share things about my personal life: about my wife and my children, pictures of my dog and cat, the performance of the best football team on Merseyside. I'll talk about that film I watched over the weekend or that box set that I'm hooked on or that book that inspired me.

I also think we need to be mindful of the personal things we should probably not share, like the fact that we are going on holiday soon or are excited for the weekend. Some children don't get to go on holidays or won't be excited about being off school. For some, that Friday feeling is one of anxiety, dread and the threat of hunger, or worse. So just be a little careful about sharing those things. Be sensitive and, because you are learning to know your children well, you'll know what to share, what to avoid and when. Connect on a human as well as a professional level, and allow them to know you well too. You will soon see how they are learning to relate to you and to each other with all the benefits that true connection brings.

EVERY CHILD (AND ADULT) NEEDS A CHAMPION

It doesn't matter what role we play in school – if we are newly qualified or have been around the block a number of times – we all have our favourites. Students we just click with and who just click with us. But what about the students we find difficult to connect with? The ones who might disrupt our lessons, push us to our limits and take up most of our precious time? Surely, we can't be expected to get along with every child in the school? Of course not, we're human after all, as we have just been discussing. But you can work miracles when you pretend. Sometimes, you have to fake it until you make it.

If you treat each encounter as a teachable moment for you both – one that will leave you both more knowledgeable about the power of relationships and connection – then you will not go far wrong. After all, who needs restorative approaches if we all get along all the time? The real benefit is found in the relationships that are harder to forge and sustain.

We all need a champion and it's easy to be the champion of an easy-going, compliant child. How will you be the champion for that young person who really looks like they don't give a toss about you, about school or even about themselves? Now there is a professional challenge. The student who might resist all of your efforts is the one who may well need you the most. How can you be the teacher who cares? And I mean really cares. The one who cares authentically and unconditionally, checks in regularly with them, listens, understands, builds them up, and builds them back up when things go wrong, supports them to be the best that they can be, champions them not just inside their own classroom but in every other room in the school. This is not about rescuing children; it's about helping them be all that they can be, for themselves.

Where do we start? Remember, aim to connect with the child before you connect with the student. Seek to understand rather than to blame. Always make your own mind up about a child, don't be swayed by what your colleagues might have to say, or their reputation in the school. Catch them getting it right more than you catch them getting it wrong. Catch them in, don't catch them out, as the saying goes. Build on what they are strong at and support them in what they are struggling with. Encourage others to do the same, to see what you see. Remember, small ripples create big waves.

One more thing, in a relational school the professionals know that some students need the most love when they deserve it the least. They will ask for it in the most inappropriate ways. Be ready.

BUILD GOODWILL AT GOOD TIMES

But it's not enough to champion the children; we need to get their families on board too, and this starts with how we communicate with them. There's a whole world of difference between 'contacting parents and carers' and 'connecting with parents and carers'. By changing two letters, everything changes.

What that subtle but important change means is that we will actively seek to connect with the family, not just make contact with them when something is wrong. After all, if we only call when there is a problem with their child – or their child's behaviour – how will they feel when the school number flashes up on their phone again? What frame of mind will they be in when they answer? Will they even choose not to answer?

One school I worked with started to make a note of when children performed well or did something amazing and then, on a Friday afternoon, staff made a number of genuinely positive phone calls home to let their families know. Why Friday? Well, the idea was that children would walk in from school to a lovely greeting, something that would set them up for a great weekend ahead. Sending postcards home when children have gone the extra distance and celebrating success starts to add deposits into the relationship bank in a similar way. Sending them by post first thing on Thursday means – local delivery conditions notwithstanding – they arrive in the letterbox on Friday or Saturday and, again, the weekend is off to a great start.

Of course, these celebrations don't have to involve the time and expense of phone calls and postcards. In primary, what about having 'Positive Fridays'? All the staff can be out on the playground at the end of the day to share successes with parents and carers when they come to pick their children up. So much easier to do and more personal than making them sit through those celebration assemblies in which everyone gets a sticker, even those who clearly don't deserve it.

Remember too that building goodwill doesn't always have to be outward looking. Building it between your colleagues pays dividends too. One primary school I worked with did a wonderful thing to build and strengthen their sense of community with an approach that turned the teachers from *Guardian*-readers into guardian angels. It was quite simple (remember, relationships are simple). At no specific time and for no ulterior reason – but usually towards the end of term when staff were starting to get tired – they would unleash the angels of surprise.

The names of all the staff would go into a hat and everyone would pull out a name. They would be a guardian angel for that colleague for the whole of the following week. What made it even more special was that nobody knew who had whom: it's a secret. The angel's job was to create little surprises at various points over the week – leave a message or a joke on their desk or board to make them smile, leave their favourite magazine in their pigeonhole along with a Double Decker (what else!) or some bubble bath with a note to 'Enjoy a soak' (which is different from 'Take a bath' – language is important, as we'll discuss in Chapter 3).

Not only does this make people feel great during the week, it also builds connections. After all, the more you know about the person, the more suitable and thoughtful the surprises are. You will need to know what they like or don't like, what they appreciate or don't, what will get you the most bang for your guardian angel buck. After all, some freaks don't even like Double Deckers. These small and random acts of kindness brighten up everyone's day (giver and receiver) and can range from cheap to entirely free. It's the acts that count and, as we have already learned, little ripples make big waves.

Another school incorporated a five-minute music quiz during the Friday morning briefing. The winning person or team were awarded a bag of sweets and had someone else cover their next lunch duty. Apart from the fun and connection created in this way, playing upbeat music quite loudly at 8.00am is a sure-fire way to lift your mood and get you through to the weekend.

Another school developed badges for staff and students, but you had to get at least three nominations from staff or children to be awarded one. The badges were values-based – being kind, going above, working hard, supporting others, etc. – and given out in year group assemblies. You'd be surprised at how the staff played it down but then skipped to the front to collect their badge. The trick here is to make sure that the badges look great.

A final example of little things going a long way when it comes to building goodwill is an idea that I've heard about from lots of colleagues called 'You've been mugged'. A mug is left anonymously and unexpectedly on someone's desk with some goodies in it and a small note of appreciation for their hard work, or for going above and beyond or, even better, just because. You can add a pay-it-forward element too, meaning that it's then the recipient's turn to fill the mug and surprise a colleague. (Although we do veer back towards the 'Everyone has to get a badge, so let's think of something' celebration assemblies here …)

Building goodwill is easy and fun, and every act – no matter how little – means that there are more deposits in everyone's social capital piggy banks.

WORKING TOGETHER WORKS

Parents, carers and teachers have the same goal 99% of the time. We all want the best for the young people in our care. It's important, therefore, for teachers and parents or carers to build a relationship of their own.

As early in the year as time will allow, connecting with (as opposed to merely contacting) parents and carers either face to face, over the phone, or through a Zoom call in our new post-COVID world will pay you back many times over across the rest of the year. The purpose of the call is quite simple: to welcome the parent or carer into our community and, in doing so, establish a positive line of communication. You're investing early on in a way that will pay dividends.

Calling to praise specific examples of when a child has done well – great behaviour, a wonderful achievement, some really high-quality learning, being helpful, being a leader, being a good friend, etc. – is something you should get in early. It means that you will have the social capital in the bank with the family, which you may need to call on when things aren't going well, when you need them on your side, or when you all need to be on the same team for the sake of their child. So, only after positive calls are made and this connection is established should you call about a problem, not before. In this way, home and school have already established a trusting, workable relationship that significantly diminishes blaming, naming and shaming.

Setting up effective home–school communication and forming a team are very powerful tools in helping children to be successful. Children spend most of their lives at home and school, so when we focus on making sure we're all on the same side, our combined influence becomes very powerful indeed.

SIGNIFICANT AND IMPORTANT OTHERS

Growing up, I had two aunties: Auntie Bea and Auntie Pat. Of course, being a working-class child in the 1970s, they weren't my real aunties. But they happened to live on my row (it's now a mews) and I would see them each and every day. If you'd asked me who was in my family, I wouldn't have mentioned these two amazing ladies, but I would have mentioned my nan and my granddad, my biological aunties and uncles, and the like. But if you had asked which adults were the most *important* to me, then Auntie Bea and Auntie Pat would have been the first two names out of my mouth.

I think we throw around the term 'family' when we actually mean 'parents' or 'carers', or – as often seems the case – 'mum'. I would much prefer to talk about significant and important people in a child's life. Of course, I might not use this exact wording with children, as they might not understand it, but I would certainly ask them who they felt were the most important adults in their lives. One way of finding out who is significant to them is to ask the million-dollar question: if you won the lottery, who would you share it with? Other variations on the theme might be to ask who the last five people they texted or rang were. Or, if you got stranded in town with no money, who would you call? Or, if you had to select a football team from the adults in your life, can you name your first team? Who would you make captain and who is the ultra-dependable one you'd put in goal? Don't forget though, this isn't a literal football team, so if they start to talk about which of their cousins is the most reliable goalscorer then try to steer them back and help them see that this is a metaphor. In this way we can start to draw together a picture of who we might need to consider involving when making decisions regarding our students and/or holding meetings to better support or challenge them (with the agreement of their legal primary carer, of course).

What about you? Who would be in your significant starting XI? As my Independent Thinking friend and colleague Vic Goddard likes to say, 'Family comes in many forms' and, for me, that includes aunties who aren't aunties.[3]

---

3 V. Goddard, *The Best Job in the World* (Carmarthen: Independent Thinking Press, 2014).

UBUNTU AND RESTORATIVE COMMUNITIES

> Ubuntu is a philosophy that considers the success of the group above that of the individual.
>
> **STEPHEN LUNDIN AND BOB NELSON**[4]

At its most basic level, ubuntu is about being human, it is about being kind, it is about being compassionate, and it is about looking through the eyes of others. It fits with the philosophy of restorative practice in that it is a philosophy that puts connection, belonging and caring for each other as one community first.

Doc Rivers – the former coach of the Boston Celtics basketball team in the USA – understood that ubuntu wasn't something you did, but rather who you are and how you behave. It was what drove the team's success and, in his own words in the Netflix documentary series *The Playbook*, 'You know the old analogy of there being no "I" in team? Well, there is no "I" in ubuntu.'[5]

It's not a one-off single event or thing we do, but rather a broad set of values, beliefs, behaviours and characteristics. It's a way of life. A person can only be a person through others.

---

4   S. Lundin and B. Nelson, *Ubuntu! An Inspiring Story About an African Tradition of Teamwork and Collaboration* (New York: Broadway Books, 2010), p. 27.
5   Netflix, *The Playbook: A Coach's Rules for Life* (2020).

Barack Obama said in his 2013 eulogy for the amazing Nelson Mandela:

> *There is a word in South Africa – Ubuntu – that describes his greatest gift: his recognition that we are all bound together in ways that can be invisible to the eye.*[6]

The following story appears many times online in various forms and really struck a chord with me.

A man in South Africa was playing with a group of children. He told them he had a game for them to play and that he had hidden a basket of fruit under a tree for them to find.

'Whoever finds the basket of fruit can keep it all to themselves', he told the excited children.

In his account, he explains that what the children did next changed him forever. Instead of running off one by one, they held each other's hands and ran off together to find the fruit. When they found it, they shared it. He asked them why they did that and they told him, 'Ubuntu.'

When he asked them to explain they said, 'How can one of us be happy if all the others are sad?'

Charity may well begin at home but, if the COVID-19 pandemic lockdown has taught us anything, you will soon become lonely if that's where you stay.

In a school context, ubuntu means that we need to ask the question: what are you going to do in order to enable the community around you to improve? In this way, your sense of achievement is linked to the achievements of others, your moral obligations are determined by your responsibilities to others and the relationships we hold.

---

[6] *The Guardian*, Barack Obama's Address at Nelson Mandela's Memorial Service – in Full (10 December 2013). Available at: https://wwwtheguardian.com/world/2013/dec/10/barack-obama-nelson-mandela-memorial-service.

I can't be all I can be, unless you are all you can be.

Ubuntu is to be lived.

Restorative practice is all about the bridges, not the walls. After all, to build a bridge you need to think about more than your side of it. Modern society is plagued by sides, by fragmentation. Look at the various parties all supposedly working for the common good – schools, social services, healthcare providers, the police, the third sector, the voluntary sector, the faith sector – all so often working in silos rather than together. Despite this, as individuals we crave belonging, we want to feel connected to each other across our communities, yet can end up existing in our own homes and our own worlds, with all the emotional and mental health consequences such existential isolation can bring.

Ubuntu shows us another way.

CHAPTER 3
RESTORATIVE CONVERSATIONS AND LANGUAGE

BEHAVIOUR POLICY OR RELATIONSHIP POLICY

Can we stop talking about behaviour and start talking about relationships instead? And belonging? If we do have to have a behaviour policy, can it actually be all about learning and achievement? (Sure, we can put 'behaviour policy' on the cover to keep the inspectors happy.)

In a restorative school, the number one focus is always the relationships. In this way, we not only address misbehaviour in a way that strengthens relationships, but also – if harm has been done to another, physically or mentally – we can focus on the harm done, rather than just homing in on the rule-breaking.

What follows are my golden rules when it comes to addressing behaviour in a restorative way. It is not simple, but I've tried to make this list as simple as possible:

- Establish policies that ensure a safe place for learning. Real safety, however, comes from fostering and maintaining caring relationships.
- Misbehaviour needs to be seen as having an impact on people and relationships. It's not just about rule-breaking and systems.

- If we see misbehaviour as a symptom, then our policies need to address the root causes. We need to ask ourselves: what is really going on here? What are we being told? Remember, too, the causes of misbehaviour may well be numerous and multifaceted and should be addressed by all members of the school community equally in a way that asserts high levels of challenge within a highly supportive environment (more on this shortly).

- Students, staff and anyone else directly affected should be at the centre of the process, with their needs addressed first.

- Those indirectly affected might include other students, other teachers, parents and members of the wider community.

- Policies should be co-written and co-produced by everyone they will impact. In this way you will ensure the best possible chance of everyone heading in the same direction and creating the consistency that needs to be shown by all, especially the adults.

Another important factor here is that any behaviour policy that highlights this restorative and relational approach to behaviour needs to be short enough for people to read, easy for people to communicate and then be relentlessly over-communicated.

If you want a simple rule about this then follow my simple packed lunch principle – the policy should never weigh more than a sandwich and not take longer to read than that sandwich takes to eat.

RESTORATIVE CONVERSATIONS AND LANGUAGE

THE POWER OF 'WITH'

If you're flicking through this book and have happened to chance upon this section, then it's your lucky day as I want to introduce what is effectively the cornerstone of restorative practice. And it all revolves around one four-letter word.

What I want to share with you is a model originally created by Daniel Glaser,[1] but more recently promoted and adapted by Ted Wachtel and Paul McCold.[2] It's called the 'social discipline window' and it's the basis for a powerful and transformative restorative practice model that is built on the twin pillars of high challenge and high support. (Actually, the original version uses the word 'control', but I prefer the word 'challenge' for reasons that will become clear.)

It's a little philosophical, but the way we do things around here. It's a way of being in our relationships, rather than a way of doing.

This model shows to us that there are always four ways of working with our students, our colleagues and the wider school community.

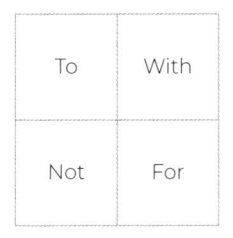

To	With
Not	For

SOURCE: **ADAPTED FROM WACHTEL AND McCOLD, RESTORATIVE JUSTICE IN EVERYDAY LIFE (2008), P. 124.**

---

1. D. Glaser, *The Effectiveness of a Prison and Parole System* (Indianapolis, IN: Bobbs-Merrill, 1969).
2. T. Wachtel and P. McCold, Restorative Justice in Everyday Life. In H. Strang and J. Braithwaite (eds), *Restorative Justice and Civil Society* (Cambridge: Cambridge University Press, 2008), pp. 114–129.

Take a moment to consider carefully each of these ways of working with others. In which quadrant do you think you are currently spending most of your time? Where does the culture in your school or organisation expect you to be focusing your energies? What would happen if you approached your work in each of the four different ways? How would things change? If part of the teacher's role is to build and strengthen healthy and nourishing relationships, that will allow young people to grow into positive and independent adults, where should we be spending our time?

Clearly, no one wants to put their hands up and admit to doing nothing at all for the children they teach. Although it happens.

Doing things *to* them is common in schools, especially ones of a more draconian, authoritarian nature. You'll no doubt recognise this behaviour. 'You need this for the exam so just get it written down and learn it. End of.'

Doing things *for* them is also common in schools, especially ones that are full of loving and caring adults. You'll no doubt recognise this too. 'Ah, don't worry, you did your best, give it here …'

And what about *with*? When have you done things in partnership *with* the children and young people? A genuine mutually beneficial learning experience that has you working together, not quite as equals, but each with something to bring, something to share and something to learn?

Of course, doing things *with* takes time. Doing things *for* or *to* young people saves time and are acts born out of a combination of the pressures teachers are under to 'get stuff done' as well as, often, a genuine desire to see children succeed (at the expense of the benefits of failing and learning to keep trying). And of course, not doing anything takes no time at all, but it does last a lifetime. It's the gift that keeps on giving.

At this point, let's refine our model by adding two more elements that help teachers make the shift to the *with* box: the twin issues of 'challenge' and 'support'.

When we say 'challenge', we don't mean confrontation. We mean behaviours that set the rules (yes, rules are important in restorative practice too), limits and expectations of how we behave around here. There are consequences to actions, we outline concerns openly and honestly, and we encourage responsibility and accountability.

When we say 'support', we don't mean packages of support – interventions and so on. We mean behaviours that are encouraging, that show empathy and offer nurture, that are compassionate, kind and respectful. We position ourselves alongside students when they need us.

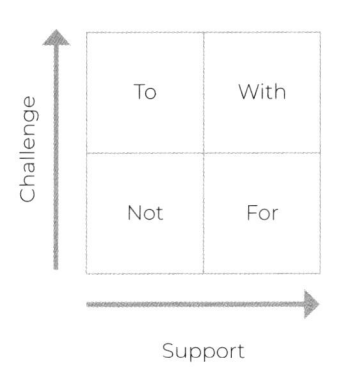

	Challenge	
	To	With
	Not	For

Support

SOURCE: ADAPTED FROM WACHTEL AND McCOLD, RESTORATIVE JUSTICE IN EVERYDAY LIFE (2008), P. 124.

Again, now think about your colleagues, your own experiences of school and, with honesty, your own professional moments in all four boxes.

Low challenge, low support means we're in the *not* box. 'This is Mr Jones, your supply teacher, and here is a worksheet to do.' 'When you finish your work, you can colour it in.' 'If you just sit quietly we can get through to the bell.' 'Today we're going to watch a DVD …' And remember, it's not just how we act with children that we are looking at here; it's how we treat each other too. When a colleague says to you, 'Your Year 5s were awful in assembly today', they are in the *not* box. No challenge, no support, just blame.

Wachtel and McCold labelled the *not* box 'neglectful'. Strong perhaps, but fair? Often, yes – the words lazy, wrong job, salary stealer, not interested, passenger might spring to mind, and, yes, teachers like this do exist. I've been in enough staffrooms and led enough INSET sessions to know that. Every job has them. But I think that there are two more layers to this box, which are worthy of a little more understanding.

I think that we can all admit to ending up in this box, despite ourselves, when we are feeling tired, burnt out, wrung out or hung out to dry by the system, when we lack confidence, when we are ill-equipped or under-trained, or when we don't have enough time. While our genuinely neglectful colleagues need a farewell party and a gold watch so the children can get something better, if we find ourselves in the *not* box for these reasons, we are usually crying out for more support, more nurturing, a tad more empathy and maybe even a little more challenge. Sometimes teachers end up in the *not* box as the result of poor leadership: practice is allowed to not only slip there (it happens) but remain there, unchallenged. If you've ever fumed as old Tom sits at the back of the hall during an INSET day doing the *Guardian* crossword instead of seeking to improve his practice, then you will know what I mean.

If you find yourself in the top left-hand corner, then you're in the *to* box. The challenge is high, 'I want this done by Monday morning …' but the support is low '… as that's this week's homework. Detention if you don't do it.' In the *to* box, students have boundaries and high expectations in place, but we don't get alongside them to offer the right support or help. It is a box that creates compliance but with very little ownership. 'I'll do it, but only because you make me.' 'I'll behave, but only when you're around.'

What do drivers do when they are approaching speed cameras (other drivers, not you, obviously)? Yep, that's right, they (you) slow down. Why? Is it because they have suddenly understood the error of their ways and turned over a new, slower, leaf? Nah. It's because they don't want to get caught. They don't want the three points on their licence. They don't want the expense of the fine or of the increased insurance premium. They might not mind breaking the law, but they don't want to be caught. And what do you (sorry, they) do once they've gone past the camera? That's right, they put the pedal back to the metal and they're back on their speedy way.

In the *to* box, the teachers make like a speed camera. Children will say and do all the right things when the teacher is around but their behaviour will revert the minute they leave their sight. They were never doing the right thing because it was the right thing, but rather because they were told – with an overt or covert threat of sanction – what to do. It makes it look like you're running a great school, but really it's all about compliance.

Wachtel and McCold used the words 'authoritarian' and 'punitive' to describe behaviours typical of this style of practice.[3] Strong perhaps, but fair? Yes, but maybe not always. Sometimes – especially with older children – there does need to be the occasional 'just knuckle down and get it done', not in the name of compliance but as a move towards independence (of which more shortly). This won't stretch their ability but will build responsibility.

In the bottom right-hand corner is low challenge and high support: cuddle and muddle. In this classroom you are more likely to make excuses than progress. It's a potentially unsafe environment with neither boundaries nor expectations, in which children are supported but not held to account for their actions. It's a situation in which you are asking for trouble, sometimes in the form of spoon-feeding children their learning. They might love being in this box to start with, but it won't last. Wachtel and McCold described the *for* box as 'permissive'.[4] You're there for the right reasons – because you genuinely want children to do well and you genuinely care for them – but, ultimately, you will do more harm than good. 'Hi, kids, call me Dave.'

The top right-hand box is the domain that is built on high challenge and high support. 'This is a tricky one. If you get stuck I can give you a few pointers, but no more!' 'The way you did that was great, and to make it even better next time you could try this.' Wachtel and McCold used the terms 'restorative', 'collaborative' and 'reintegrative' to describe the winning approach of being in the *with* box.[5]

There are monsters lurking in the other three quadrants, but in the *with* box, 'ere be relationships: relationships built

---

3 Wachtel and McCold, Restorative Justice in Everyday Life, p. 117.
4 Wachtel and McCold, Restorative Justice in Everyday Life, p. 117.
5 Wachtel and McCold, Restorative Justice in Everyday Life, p. 117.

on trust and real connection. In my experience, this approach is the one that creates genuinely independent learners – students who learn to self-manage, motivate themselves, and take responsibility for and, importantly, control over their own behaviours. In a nutshell, it creates students who aren't part of the audience, they are part of the cast. Or, as a school in Leeds that I've worked with says, they're not passengers but part of the crew.

It is my aim to be practising as much as I possibly can in the top right-hand box – holding students and colleagues to high standards of behaviour, while at the same time providing the support and encouragement necessary for them to meet these expectations. It is me ensuring that no decisions are made without the input of the people they will affect. This is the relational approach, which is at the heart of restorative practice. In this way, you can be authoritative, but not authoritarian.

I've had lots of interesting discussions about the words 'authoritative' and 'authoritarian'. Aren't they the same thing, as is often said? Authoritative teachers guide their students and tend to adjust their expectations to the needs of the child (working *with*), while still being in a position of authority. They have explicit expectations for behaviour, but offer nurture, compassion, kindness and empathy to enable children to meet their high expectations. An authoritative classroom follows the school rules while taking individual students' needs into consideration. An authoritative teacher keeps to the rules but works hard to support children to follow them. Rules and expectations are important, but they are adjusted to meet the needs of the child. Consequences are logical; teachers are kind and involved. Authoritarian teachers and leaders, however, tend to want to control through power. They exert power over their students (working *to*). They tend to be strict and work on the principle that the rules should be followed 'because I said so'. School rules keep everything in place and if they are broken, a punishment will follow. Rules are absolute; authoritarian leaders are cold and less involved.

Working restoratively isn't about having less authority; it has everything to do with how you exercise that authority. 'With' – that little word – is the key. An authoritative approach holds tenaciously to the school's values and challenges members of the community to demonstrate these values in all their interactions. And I mean all. Everything counts.

So, in which box do you spend most of your time? When things aren't going your way, which box do you default to? Be honest. After all, when we are reactive, our behaviour is often emotional and unconsidered. When we take the time to think about our actions, we can be more effective – thinking and behaving on purpose. For example, we often default to the *to* box when things go wrong. Rather than seeking to understand, we seek to blame. When we do, we look for who is at fault, what rule has been broken and what punishment fits the crime.

I can't tell you how many times I've thought about what box I'm in as a dad, as a friend and, especially, as a husband. The truth is, no matter what relationship dynamic you reflect on, you will have spent time in all four boxes.

Let me take you back to chez Finnis for another slice-of-life example. Watching my son changing his sheets is hard work for me, particularly when he gets to the duvet. You see, the way I do it is to turn the duvet cover inside out and line the top corners up with the top corners of the duvet (hands inside the duvet cover), grab the corners, flip the cover the right way round (trapping the duvet in the process), give it a shake and then go to the bottom corners, put the corners of the duvet in the corners of the cover, give it another shake and do the buttons up along the bottom. Job's a good 'un. Now, I've shown my son a few times but he thinks the better way is to start with the duvet cover the right way round and get inside it with the duvet, pinning the corners before drawing himself out. But often, when he starts to reverse out of the duvet cover, the duvet comes with him. And if the dog spots this, he's in there too! I've learned to just shut the door and leave him to it. After all, he gets there in the end. My urge is to go to the *for* box as that's quick and easy and, I tell myself, at least it'll be done properly. Is he doing it properly though? Yes, just in his own way, not mine. Do you ever do things for students or your own loved ones because you want to know they've been done properly?

Of course, there are times when a fly on the wall in our home would find me in the *to* box. If I come home, after a 12-hour day, to two pairs of shoes by the back door rather than in the shoe cupboard, well, talk about hitting the roof. And if I head into the kitchen and there's a cup in the sink rather than in the dishwasher, well, that's it. I'm in that *to* box and I'm ranting and raging about whose mess this is and how it had better get cleaned up quick. What I'm talking about here is how becoming reactive and emotional pulls or pushes me into the *to* box and, after all, it isn't always what you do but how you do it. An emotionally unregulated dad will struggle to help regulate a child. An unregulated teacher will struggle to help emotionally regulate a student.

But, like all good fathers, every now and then, I get it right. When my daughter was learning to tie her shoelaces, we spent some time on a Sunday afternoon with one of those books with laces on the cover. She had her shoe on her knee and there was music playing in the background. The Sunday roast was cooking away merrily. You know, it was one of those roasts with the potatoes that end up just right. I'm sure I spotted Nigella with her face pressed to the window looking in enviously. And, of course, the shoelace tying went brilliantly.

Monday morning comes and I'm proudly turning on my 'world's best father' mode, thinking, 'Yep, I'm high on challenge and high on support and high on that feeling of being firmly in the *with* box.'

'No, darling, I'm not putting your shoes on for you.' My voice is at its nurturing best. 'Remember, what we agreed?' I continue, 'Remember the lesson yesterday? The music? The potatoes? We agreed you're going to do it yourself today.' She sits on the bottom step and I'm giving her all the encouragement a doting father can. 'You can do it, that's brilliant.'

Then I look at my watch.

Before long, Nigella is a distant dream and, like a robot in an Amazon warehouse, I'm shifting boxes. The challenge is still high, but the support is waning. My tone has changed and I'm saying things like, 'Can you hurry?! We're going to be late.' My non-verbals have changed too, in subtle but noticeable ways. Of course, rather than tie the lace quickly she starts to panic. The *to* box is making things worse and I could go back to the *with* box – indeed, I should – but I look at my watch again.

Now I'm heading straight for the *for* box. I do not pass go. I do not pick up £100. Nigella is on the phone to social services and I'm angrily doing her laces *for* her. Defeat snatched from the jaws of victory in true Everton FC style.

To make matters worse, a few days later we had a family trip to the *not* box and now she heads off to school each morning with her shoes stubbornly held in place by Velcro. That sound you hear when she takes her new lace-less shoes off, that's her heart breaking just a little bit more each day.

I know you are judging my parenting style and thinking, if he can't be relational with one child, how am I supposed to manage it with hundreds? But I do want to illustrate that even with one little girl who I love to bits and who loves me equally (for now) – and with such a simple task as putting shoes on – even I can't stay in the *with* box, especially when I'm short of time and under pressure. How many times in your working day do you find yourself short of time and under pressure? That's why this theory is easy to learn, but not so easy to live (I told you relationships were hard). However, all is not lost. The more of your colleagues you can get into the *with* box, the easier it becomes.

The model can be used to describe and understand *all* relationships. It can be overlaid into teaching, pastoral support, social care, leadership and, if you're a parent reading this, yes, parenting too. Over the years I've developed the ambition to get into the *with* box for as much of the day as possible. Some days I do well. Some days I don't visit it enough. Some days I trip up over my daughter's laces. It's all about continual improvement – lots of 1%s, remember – and having the bravery and commitment to encourage feedback from those around me to let me know how I'm doing.

DON'T BE AFRAID OF THE 'L WORD'

> Twenty-five years of neurobiological research tells us that children learn best when they feel loved.
>
> DR ANDREW CURRAN[6]

The L word matters. And, as the saying goes, love is a verb: it's what you do. So, how can we show love consistently and effectively, each and every day, with every student?

Well, a great start is to simply bring yourself to work. Not just your professional self but your authentic self. We have already discussed the idea of sharing a little of yourself: your personal life and feelings. All of these little acts count and all the more so when you show up like you mean it, when you are true to who you are, not hiding behind a mask or pretending to be someone else.

Follow your own style and personality, always. If you aren't that all-singing, all-dancing, jazz hands type of teacher then that's perfectly OK. There is no need to fake it. The teacher next door may well be like that, and be going down a storm with the Year 8s, but that doesn't matter. 'To thine own self be true,' as Shakespeare wrote.[7] 'I see your true colours shining through,' as Cyndi Lauper sang.[8] Not every student (or inspector) relates to that style anyway, and they will want to connect with you for different reasons. Furthermore, don't pretend to like certain music,

---

6 See https://www.independentthinking.co.uk/associates/dr-andrew-curran/.
7 *Hamlet*, Act 1, Scene 3.
8 True Colors, from the album of the same name (Epic Records, 1986).

films or trends. You will be found out, like that time you used the word 'hood' to describe the leafy cul-de-sac you live on.

Using students' names is crucial when it comes to showing that you care. Pronouncing their names correctly shows that you really care, no matter how difficult it is to learn and remember them all. Addressing them by name each time you see them shows that you are acknowledging who they are and helps build that all-important connection. This is particularly important to get right for children with unusual (to white, western ears) names.[9] If you don't know how to pronounce their name, just ask them, and practise saying it until you get it right. Another way to build a connection is to ask students what they would like you to call them, but don't come up with a nickname or abbreviation to make life easier for you.

You'd also be amazed at how far giving compliments go. Do it genuinely and consistently, with everyone. What's more, shower compliments all around school and not just in your classroom. Be that teacher who compliments students on how smart they look, not the one who only ever comments on their appearance when asking them to tuck in their shirt. This is a great example of 'catching them in, not catching them out', as we touched on earlier. Dole them out for pieces of work (especially ones outside of your subject area or class), academic, sporting or artistic achievements – anything to which students have applied themselves beyond the bare minimum. Giving compliments is just a basic way to help them feel good about themselves and about you, to make them smile (even if only on the inside, it still counts) and, yes, to show love.

---

[9] See, for example, R. Kohli and D. G. Solórzano, Teachers, Please Learn Our Names! Racial Microaggressions and the K-12 Classroom, *Race Ethnicity and Education* 15(4) (2012): 441-462, DOI: 10.1080/13613324.2012.674026.

Linked to the giving of compliments is celebrating students' achievements with them. If you hear another teacher or child talking about a student's achievements, seek them out and congratulate them. These students don't even have to be in your year or class. Think about what it's like when people congratulate you and how great that feels.

Asking students questions counts too. It shows that you are interested in them beyond the world of teaching and learning. What music are you listening to? Do you have any TV recommendations? Did you have a good evening? How are you doing today? How are you feeling about the weekend? What do you have planned? How did football/netball practice go? Did the rehearsals go well? These questions are aimed at showing interest and sparking conversations that show you want to know more about them.

Try to keep positive and upbeat with your students. Consistency of mood is important, and it builds trust and reduces stress. Once you have built a connection you can let your occasional bad days show a little more and they will respect that and even try to help you. Just don't ever take your bad days out on them, that's what NQTs are for (joke). And if you are having a particularly tough day, remember that some of our students – David, for example, who we met in Chapter 1 – have got it tougher than us. Tomorrow we'll probably have a better day, but they might not. The simplest thing is to remember to smile. Remember how contagious a smile is. A real smile can trick the brain into thinking that things aren't too bad, which can improve our mood, let alone that of those around us. It's not about being happy all the time; it's about being positive.

Time outs and check-ins with groups of students during tough times – exams, transitions, the approach of the school holidays, Monday mornings, Friday afternoons and the likes – show you care. Being present ensures we will not miss those crucial moments when students really need us. By 'being present', I mean listening to students – really listening. That means being in the room with them mentally as well as physically, not catching up on your admin while they're talking to you. Students want to be heard and listened to actively. It can be difficult for students to bring their concerns to an adult, so make sure you take a genuine 'time out' to really listen to them. Listening to someone shows that we are interested in them. And who knows? We could be the only person who listens, really listens, to that child. Do you know what the secret of great listening is? It's to listen with the intent to understand, not to respond.

Finally, check you are sharing your love equally with all your students. Make sure you are showing interest, compassion and love with each and every one of them. Do all you can to ensure that no student walks into your classroom without being acknowledged, whether that's through simple eye contact (that teacher trait of having eyes in the back of our heads is great for this) or saying the student's name at least once. That simple connection and showing of interest will go a long way. In this way, we make sure that no child falls through the cracks and goes unnoticed, that every child is seen and knows that they matter to you.

So, let's spread love. Spread it as thick as my mum spreads butter – and love.

The little things, well, they aren't that little.

LABELS BELONG ON JARS

The language we use creates the reality we experience. Does our language serve to build and strengthen relationships with our students and across our school communities? Becoming conscious of the power our language has – and using that power deliberately for relational purposes – will have a positive impact on the quality of our relationships and, thus, on everyone around us.

How often have you heard yourself or your colleagues talking about that 'hard to reach' child? Or that 'difficult to engage' class? Do those epithets smack of possibility or defeat? Of growth or closure? And who do those statements blame? With language like that, you've lost the match before you've even kicked the ball. But what happens if you change your descriptions? What if 'hard to reach' became 'that child who I've been unable to build a relationship with yet'? What if 'difficult to engage' became 'I haven't found a way to ignite their spark yet'? Does that change the experience, the sense of challenge, the possibility of different possibilities? Remember the power of 'yet'.[10]

Let's try some more.

> 'Challenging behaviour'? How about 'distressed behaviour'?
>
> 'They're just plain lazy'? How about asking 'what's stopping them from finishing'?
>
> 'Can't behave' or 'won't behave'?
>
> 'Unacceptable behaviour'? Could you try 'understandable behaviour'?

---

10 C. S. Dweck, The Power of Yet [video], *TEDxNorrköping* (12 September 2014). Available at: https://www.youtube.com/watch?v=J-swZaKN2Ic.

'Difficult child'? Maybe 'child with difficulties' will get you further?

'That family's trouble'? What about 'the family that is currently having troubles'?

Let's keep going.

'Autistic child' or 'child with autism'? See the child first.

'Learning difficulty' or 'teaching difficulty'?

'Attention seeking' or 'attention needing'?

'Case file' or 'child's file'?

'LAC' or 'child who is looked after'? Abbreviations are great for sandwiches; I love a BLT.

'Difficult class' or 'class having difficulties'?

'They are kicking off again' or 'Mark is struggling at the moment and I can see that he is a little distressed'?

'They won't behave' or 'they need help to be able to behave'?

The only label we should give a student is their name. Changing one piece of language might not change the world, but it could change the world for one student.

'I'm so sick of Eliza, I'm glad when she isn't in my class. I'm not having her back in my lesson until she is ready to learn!' Notice how the language places all the onus on the student. But we're the professional. They're just the young person who is not yet emotionally or neurologically mature. As Dr Curran, who we met earlier, once told me, 'You can't be older than your brain.' So, what if we used different language here? A good starting point is to reframe the statement as a question. You don't have to know the answer straight away, but at least a question gives you options, possibilities, the chance of victory. In the case of

Eliza, how about: 'What can I do differently, so that she wants to come back into my lesson to learn?' Notice how that shifts the focus and helps to at least share the responsibility.

The golden rule in all of this is to separate the deed from doer, the act from the actor. I've worked with children and young people who have committed criminal offences, but I've never worked with a 'young offender'. In this way, you can focus on the behaviour while still valuing the person. Even adults feel attacked by criticism that challenges their whole identity rather than their behaviour, so imagine how a child feels.

'When you arrive late, I get worried' opens up a very different conversation than 'You're late! See me at the end of the lesson.' You're not letting the unacceptable behaviour slide, but you are addressing it in a way that keeps building and strengthening relationships front and centre. That's the restorative way.

Of course, sometimes our pernicious passion for labels transcends words. We have a whole drawer full of acronym labels to stick on troublesome children, don't we? Bear that in mind next time you hear colleagues talking about the number of LACs on FSMs.[11] I don't struggle with children who are looked after – surely we hope all children are looked after, whether we mean in a family or in foster placements (maybe we drop the placement; after all, I place a drink on a table, not a child)? A PRU is a school – another sort of school, but still a school.

Language is a great tool for subconsciously guiding our thoughts too. It's what hypnotists do all the time. If you and I sit down for a meeting and my opening line is 'This is going to be a really difficult meeting', where does that

---

11 Looked-after-children on free school meals, for those not fluent in edu-acronyms.

lead your thoughts? 'OK, Year 11 – we all know that this is going to be a tough year for you' might be true, but it's hardly St Crispin's Day revisited, is it? Note too, that negatives don't exist as far as our brains are concerned. 'Don't think about …' is just another way of saying 'Think about …' Telling children, 'Don't get stressed' before their exams means that all they really hear and focus on is the word 'stressed'. 'Don't talk to strangers' and we start to wonder why not and who these people might be. 'Don't worry, be happy' sends out all types of mixed messages, even in song.

It's a minefield, I know, but the three-step process by which our thoughts impact on our relationships is quite simple really (remember, relationships are simple):

1 Thoughts to language.

2 Language to reality.

3 Reality to relationships.

What's in a word? Everything. So, save those labels for your spice rack.

THE RESTORATIVE CHAT

Often, good restorative conversations are nothing more than a series of small chats. Not big sit-down talks but smaller, almost inconsequential conversations. Not held formally around a table, but brief, side-by-side chats as you walk down the corridor together or queue up to get your lunch.

Your mum was right, God gave us two ears and one mouth for a reason. The secret to being a great listener is to spend less time talking than we do listening. And, if we are talking, it should be to ask great questions: questions that stimulate enquiry, probe for understanding and promote genuine dialogue. There will be times when we need to have more structured, and more serious, conversations, but it helps if we lay the foundations by building the habit of talking *and* listening.

MORE QUESTIONS AND FEWER ANSWERS

When conflict occurs in school – as it naturally will – we need to give students and staff opportunities to have the best possible chance of getting back on track. They need:

- A chance to tell their side of the story – their unique perspective and account of what happened.

- The chance to express their thoughts and feelings – again from their perspective.

- An opportunity to understand the perspectives of others and the impact of the behaviour in question on everyone.

- The space to think about how to prevent a reoccurrence of the behaviour.

- The opportunity to accept responsibility for the harm caused.

- The space to identify what needs everyone has.

- The chance to come up with a plan to meet these needs and move forward.

- The chance to explore issues of reintegration as part of moving forward.

Once we know what these non-negotiables are, we can really get down to business.

As we move forward with our restorative modelling it is important to remember to help students reflect more, something we can achieve by asking thinking and feeling questions. In this way we make clearer the link between thoughts, emotions and actions, something that, in turn, increases connectedness and kindness and emotional intelligence, in all its many facets. Like the unsent angry email, if you express it, you feel it – and if you feel it, you're more likely to move on. By taking this approach, one that spends less time looking at the problem and more looking for the solution – less time looking to the past and more looking towards the future – we have a genuine opportunity to decrease conflicts and disruptions and encourage forgiveness. After all, as the saying goes, if you change the way you look at things, the things you look at will start to change.

DIFFICULT CONVERSATIONS, DO THEY HAVE TO BE?

Have you ever been really cross, annoyed or hurt? Tell me about it! No, really, tell me how you feel.

How many times have you been affected by someone else's behaviour but never told them? Restorative practice is, as you know by now, all about high challenge and high support, and we can use this simple (remember, relationships are simple) framework in the conversations we have with all members of our community.

The following statement structures can be used to challenge or support someone's behaviour, to highlight their strengths, to encourage and nurture them, as well as to hold them to account when they have overstepped your boundaries or fallen short of your expectations. They are 'affective' statements, which means they involve an emotional response – rather than a purely rational one – and are drawn from the work of Dr Marshall Rosenberg in his book *Nonviolent Communication*.[12] They can be used with students, colleagues, families and other agencies as and when necessary.

Dr Rosenberg suggests a simple (that word again, I told you) yet highly effective four-step language construct:

1 Behaviour.

2 Impact.

3 Needs.

4 Requests.

In this model, the first step is to name the behaviour. We get to share our unique perspective: it might be about something we've seen, something we've heard, something that's left us feeling a certain way. We need to be very specific, avoiding generalisations in our language. In other words, we don't use words like 'always', 'never', 'everyone', 'all', 'nobody'. These are all words that set the restorative overgeneralisation klaxon off.

'You're always late', 'You never bring your homework', 'You are all so rude', 'Everyone treats me this way', etc. If you use this type of language, you give others wiggle room to cut your argument off at the knee, like King Arthur meeting the Black Knight, as they point out the one time they did bring their homework. 'It's just a flesh wound …'

---

12 M. B. Rosenberg, *Nonviolent Communication: A Language of Compassion* (Encinitas, CA: PuddleDancer Press, 1999).

Instead, we need to ensure that our language is very specific and delivered in a way that comes across as firm but caring, never pedantic. In this way, 'You're always late' becomes 'You were late this morning'; 'You never bring your homework' becomes 'This is the third time this term you haven't brought your homework'; 'You're all so rude' becomes 'When you tap your ruler on the table like that it interrupts the class'; and so on. Of course, this also works when we are reinforcing positive behaviour. For example, 'You're always helpful' becomes 'I saw you supporting your friend today'; 'You never have a problem with reading' becomes 'You read so well today'.

The important thing here is, again, to separate the deed – good or bad – from the doer; the act – constructive or destructive – from the actor. Note, though, that we mustn't make that separation so wide that people don't take responsibility. However, we must ensure that we challenge the behaviour while valuing the person. As I mentioned earlier, it's much easier to alter a small aspect of our behaviour than it is our whole self.

So, we start with clearly and specifically naming the behaviour at issue. Relationships are central to everything we do, and we want to be as clear as possible about the behaviour we are challenging or reinforcing. This allows us to take account of different perspectives and to tease out any differences in versions of events. After all, when it comes to the truth, there's always at least three versions: my truth, your truth and *the* truth.

In the second step we move from 'behaviour' to 'impact'. What has been the impact of the behaviour, the act, the event, on relationships and on people? This is where we start to employ 'I' statements. When a statement begins with 'I feel ...', we own that statement, that emotion. This is a much more constructive and helpful sentence than one that begins, 'You make me feel …' The word 'make' puts us in the realm of naming and blaming. It is also empowering to the person describing their feelings. No one is making me do anything. 'I feel …' means I have control over me; you do not dictate my feelings.

So, in this way, addressing issues about lateness start with 'I feel worried about you when you arrive late', 'I feel frustrated when you tap your ruler on the table like that', 'I feel inspired when I read your piece of work', 'When you stayed back and helped me tidy the books, I felt really supported.' The focus here is on the impact on you and the relationship. Notice the huge relational difference between, 'You made me really disappointed by getting kicked out of your science lesson again' and 'When I heard you were sent out of science for the second time this week, I felt disappointed because we had discussed how things were going to be different.' To build on this further, you can also explain why you feel the way you do – for example, 'I feel frustrated because I'm trying to give out the instructions for the next task, but your tapping ruler is causing a distraction.'

Of course, the 'I' statements don't mean that you need to bare your soul and leave yourself vulnerable. There is a risk that someone will repeat the behaviour if they know how it has impacted on you because they want to wind you up. The aim is for mutually supportive rather than antagonistic relationships, but of course that takes time. Your disclosures have got to be thought through and balanced – especially early on in the process – but if we don't let people know how their behaviour affects us, how will they ever know?

In the third step, we start to think about the solution and what needs to happen for us to arrive at it successfully. Once we have identified our needs, we are better able to communicate them effectively. 'I feel frustrated when you tap your ruler on the table like that, so I need you to put your ruler down, please', 'I feel disappointed because we discussed how things were going to be different, so I need you to stay in your lessons.' Without step 3 we have carefully described a problem but there is no sense of moving beyond that and no agreement regarding what solving the problem looks like.

Once we have agreement we can move onto step 4: the request for agreement, the invitation for that need to be met. 'Would you be willing to put your ruler away?' 'Are you prepared to stay in your lessons?' 'I need you to take your seat now, so would you be willing to do that?'

Bear in mind too, as we look at the power of language, the non-verbal elements of communication. Has anyone ever told you, 'It wasn't what you said, it was how you said it'? If they have, in future you might want to consider your tone. Non-verbals, including tone of voice, are so important. A calm voice with a lowered tone – hands on your lap or by your side – sends a very different message than an all-shouting, all-gesticulating delivery does. Sitting alongside someone, especially if they are a great deal smaller than you, can make all the difference. Eye contact and facial expressions also play a massive part in how we communicate, especially if we take cultural differences into account and act accordingly.

Conversations about feelings are always difficult, and telling someone about the impact their actions have on you is always hard. If the other party isn't aware that certain behaviours have an impact on you, how can they change them? Punishment won't help them to be aware of the consequences of their behaviour (beyond the fact that the behaviour elicits a punishment) or, more importantly from a restorative perspective, the impact it might be having on others.

One final word on these kinds of restorative conversations: they work best when you have plenty of social capital deposited in the bank. Without that, these carefully structured statements land very differently. Without a relationship, why would someone care so much? With great relationships, who wouldn't want the opportunity to put it right and get back on track?

BUILD BRIDGES, NOT BRICK WALLS

When relationships break down and we need to look to restore them, it's important to consider the power of language and how we use it for good, not evil. The words we use and the conversations we have are the keys to making an alternative future a genuine possibility.

At their heart, these conversations need to encourage us to shift the power, to move the dynamic from an emphasis on punishment and retribution to a more powerful restorative one that puts the community first. We do this through using effective questions that generate productive dialogues, helping us to move beyond the past to consider the present and then build a better future. It is a journey that takes us from seeking to blame to a place where we are seeking to understand.

As a starting point, remember that, as Stephen Covey says, 'The way we see the problem *is* the problem.'[13] In other words, are we focusing on problems or possibilities? Are

---

13 S. R. Covey, *The 7 Habits of Highly Effective People: Powerful Lessons in Personal Change* (New York: Simon & Schuster, 2004), p. 40.

our conversations and dialogues about fear and fault or opportunities, strengths and solutions? Does the language we use stigmatise and blame? Does it shift responsibility from us to others? Do we see the people involved as part of the problem or part of the solution? Is everyone at the meeting part of the cast, or are some merely members of the audience? Are children passengers or are they crew? By changing our language, we can start to change the way we see the problem.

How often do we think we've asked the right question and then been surprised by the answer that comes back? Or think we've said the right thing and get an unexpected and unwanted reaction? Maybe it's not the response that's wrong, it's our input? Garbage in, garbage out, as the old computing adage goes. The better the question, the more chance it has to alter the thinking and, consequently, the behaviour, of all concerned.

Don't say …	**Instead say …**
Why did you do it?	Can you share with me what happened?
Can you tell me the truth?	What is your view of what happened?
Who is to blame for what happened?	Who has been affected by what happened? What was the impact on you and on others?
You need to think about your behaviour.	What would you like to see happen? What does that look like for you?

Don't say ...	Instead say ...
You need to do X.	What ideas do you have that would meet both our needs? (The key part of this question is 'both our needs'.)
Who else is to blame?	Have you tried to look at what happened from another perspective?

Changing 'why' to 'what' will always help. And a question is usually better than an order or an accusation. Questions require engagement answers don't.

THE RESTORATIVE FIVE

It can be helpful to have a restorative model to draw on – something tried and tested to help structure your conversation. This is where the restorative five come in:

1. What happened?
2. What have your thoughts been since?
3. What are your feelings?
4. Who was affected and how were they affected?
5. What are everyone's needs when it comes to what should happen next?

Now, of course, you can't make anyone answer any of these questions: that would put you in the *to* box, not the *with* box. But they are a great set of jumping-off points for further exploration and questioning. Like all good questions, they can help us to alter our thinking and, from there, our behaviours. Questions require engagement; they need us to think, to stop for a while and reflect in a way that statements don't.

What makes these questions magic is that they keep the focus of our conversation away from both the punitive, authoritarian, blaming (*to*) conversations and the permissive, rescuing, excuse-making (*for*) conversations, instead steering us towards dialogue (*with*) that is restorative, relational and collaborative: that focuses on possibilities and the future.

THE THREE BUBBLES

Now, I'm a simple Everton supporter and if there is any way I can make things even easier, then bring it on. So, why have five restorative questions when you can have three bubbles? The three bubbles model (see page 80) makes restorative conversations even easier and more effective. Notice the timeline across the top: this is really important. Often, if you ask children what happened, they just say 'I don't know.' Taking them back to before the incident and asking what happened at that point and just afterwards can be really helpful. Minimal questions such as '... and then?' or just 'then?', 'Just before that?' and 'Just after that?' can help. Non-verbals – like a nod of the head or a hand gesture to encourage them to share a little more – can also be used to good effect.

Timeline

→

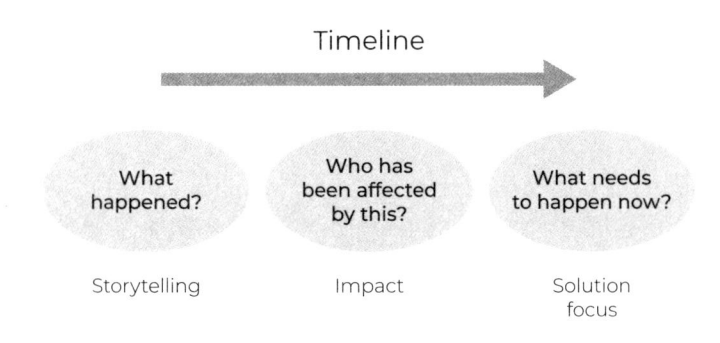

- **What happened?** — Storytelling
- **Who has been affected by this?** — Impact
- **What needs to happen now?** — Solution focus

BUBBLE 1

Bubble 1 is all about exploring what happened and ensuring that we look at this from everyone's perspective. There are as many perspectives as there are people involved – maybe more – and it is important to explore everyone's version of the truth to get to the facts. After all, the facts are what happened; our truth is true to us.

What happened?

- What happened next?
- And then?
- What has brought us here today?
- Can you tell us more about the issues that have brought us here today?
- Can you tell us more about X?
- What were your thoughts at the time?
- What were you thinking?
- What was happening before?
- What was in your head?
- What do you think about it now?
- How were you feeling?
- What else?
- After that happened, what happened next?
- At that point, what were you thinking/feeling?

So, here are lots of examples of supplementary questions to help us get to the nub of what happened, but you might notice that there is one missing – one that we tend to focus on when we work in a non-restorative way but that's actually not particularly helpful – why?

What response do you usually get when you ask a child why they have done something? Why are you late? Why haven't you brought your homework? Why are you hitting Chloe? Why have you left your PE kit at home? A shrug of the shoulders? An 'I don't know'? A 'Because they made me'? An 'I only did it because he did first'? Sound familiar? A why question is effectively a get-out-of-jail card. You've asked a question that they either don't know how to or can't answer, or they give you an answer that brings Uncle Tom Cobley and all into the bargain and now you find yourself with nowhere to go. Why questions hit brick walls, but we want questions that build bridges. The trick? Replace why questions with what questions.

There are three important areas that we need to cover with our what questions:

1 Behaviours – what happened?

2 Thoughts – what are your thoughts about what happened?

3 Feelings – what are your feelings about what happened?

We can see from bubble 1 that there are many different ways of phrasing and posing these questions. What is important to remember is that the questions should be asked in this order: we want to establish what happened first, then move onto talking about thoughts and feelings. It is important to ask the thinking questions before the feeling questions, as thinking questions can also trigger feeling responses. Feelings are vital at this stage because if you express it, you feel it, and if you feel it, you are more likely to move forward. Moving forward – not just ascertaining the facts in order to ascertain the punishment – is what restorative practice is all about.

The key thing in bubble 1 is the interrelationship between behaviours, thoughts and feelings; they are interlinked. One triggers the others. A behaviour triggers a thought which triggers a feeling. A thought can trigger a feeling which can trigger a behaviour. That's why we shouldn't underestimate the power of asking questions about each of these aspects.

With the stories told, we can move onto the next bubble.

BUBBLE 2

Bubble 2 is about exploring the impact of what's happened not on systems and policies but on people and relationships. Whereas bubble 1 explored what happened from individual perspectives, bubble 2 asks us to consider how others have been affected. It also presents an opportunity for a young person to discover the idea of unintended consequences, that the things we do may have an impact in ways we never anticipated or intended, that our actions – like dropping a pebble in a pond – cause ripples.

RESTORATIVE CONVERSATIONS AND LANGUAGE

How have you been affected?

Who else has been affected?

Anyone else?

How have others been affected?

What has been the hardest thing for you?

How do you feel now?

Who has been affected by this?

Was anyone else involved?

Can you tell us more about X?

If there was, how were they left feeling?

Has anyone else been affected by this?

Anything else to add?

If you ask a child who has been affected by what happened, who do you think the first person they say is? Yes, you're right: them. It's a good a place to start as any, so feel free to let them describe the impact on them but make sure that they don't stop there. Follow that round of questioning with, 'So (not 'but' as this can be a negative connecter) ... who else has been affected?' We might need to ask much more explicit questions, like 'So, how do you think child X was affected when that happened?', 'How was your nan affected?', and so on, dependent on the situation.

BUBBLE 3

Bubble 3 is about exploring what needs to happen next in order to move forward, what needs should be taken into consideration and how do we prevent a reoccurrence of the issue in the future. From there it is important to establish and agree on the steps that need to be taken in order to repair any harm caused.

What else needs to happen?

Can you tell us more about X?   Do you agree with that?

What do you need in order to move on from this?

What would that look like?   Are you OK with that?

What needs to happen now?   What will help you to move on from this?

When will it be done?

Anything else to add?

How does that leave you feeling?   What will it look like when it's done?

What do you think about what has been suggested?   If you can't do that, what can you do?

This final bubble, then, is all about the future. It gets us to explore what people's needs are and then come up with a plan to move the situation forward and, importantly, to stop it happening again.

The key is to ask everyone these questions individually, taking each person's request to the other parties involved and coming up with a plan that everyone agrees with. This is a crucial time in the process and it is vital that throughout you position yourself in the *with* box, and avoid the *to* or *for* boxes.

When it comes to identifying what needs to happen next, the SMARTER approach is the one to take. Your goals need to be:

    Specific

    Measurable

    Achievable

    Relevant/realistic

    Time-based

    Evaluated

    Reviewed

After all, as we saw in Chapter 2, a goal without a plan is just a wish.

When it comes to asking questions, remember to be mindful that children will often just give you the answers they think you want to hear. They will play the game they think you want them to play, they will nod at all the right times and look sad at all the right moments. If you know your students and colleagues well, you'll know when they are just saying what they think you want to hear. In my experience, the three-bubble model for holding high-quality restorative conversations means you are giving yourself the best possible chance of succeeding in your aims. Everyone gets heard and bridges are built, not burned.

One last thing to think about here – the thorny issue of the spoken apology. Even a 7-year-old has the ability to make a forced verbal apology sound like an act of aggression and we can either accept it knowing that it means nothing or open up a new front in our war of attrition with them, in which we now demand that they say sorry – and mean it! For me, the key is not to search for an apology, not at this stage anyway. Forcing the words 'I'm sorry' out of a child in the moment is counterproductive and does more harm than good. Maybe it will come later, when they actually mean it. The important thing to remember is that it's not the apology that is your goal but a changed behaviour. That's the best form of contrition in the long run, because everyone gains. The best apology is changed behaviour.

In a restorative nutshell, remember the following – 'I'm sorry' is just a statement. 'I won't do it again' is just a promise. However, 'How do I make it up to you?' is taking responsibility.

Teachers who keep one eye on the past are wise. The worry is when we keep two eyes on the past.

AN EXAMPLE FROM PRACTICE

I facilitated a restorative conference between two students in the same Year 7 class at a school in Liverpool. They had known each other since starting school, and had been friendly in the past, but ended up having a fight one day while playing football on the field. I was asked to bring them together and try to resolve the issue. I met with them both one-to-one, separately, to explore their perspectives on what had happened, their thoughts and feelings about what had led up to the fight, and if and how they could move forward. Both students spoke of wanting to sort things out, but they didn't know where to start (the beauty of restorative practice is that we can support students in opening up a dialogue and we have a structure to follow). Remember, the process is as important as the outcome of the conference.

Before our meeting, I explored with them both how I could support them by providing an opportunity to talk things through, understand the impact on each other and come up with a plan to move forward and ensure they don't have another fight. On the day, I set up the seats in a quiet space and went to get the two students.

BUBBLES 1 AND 2

Rather than laying down the ground rules, I prefer to ask what they need from each other for the conversation to go well. They agree that they might each have a different perspective, but that they will listen and search for solutions based on each other's needs. I started by asking student X to share their view of what happened, and their thoughts and feelings, before and after. I then explore bubble 2 and ask who has been affected. I then followed the same process with student Y.

The key is to get them talking with each other. 'So, student X could you share with student Y your view of what happened? You said you feel upset about what student Y said – is that something you could say a little more about?' The key is to get both students to build small bridges.

A little reflection follows. To both students: 'Can you both see the impact this has had on each other?' If they can: 'Are you ready to think about what needs to happen next?' If they are ready, then we are onto bubble 3. If not, it's important to explore bubbles 1 and 2 further.

BUBBLE 3

I asked them both what they need from each other to move forward. Then I got them to explore a plan to meet both of their needs. The risk here is we go chasing that 'I'm sorry', 'I won't do it again', 'let's shake hands and agree to be friends'. Remember that lip service is the enemy of commitment and that the best apology is changed behaviour.

The key task for me as the facilitator is to keep asking questions so that they can come up with a plan. I might need to ask, 'Are you OK with what they have suggested? If not, what do you suggest? If you can't agree to that, what could you agree to?' These are all helpful questions that keep the solution truck moving forward.

If they are struggling, I might say, 'Do you both need to take a moment? Shall we take a few minutes to reflect and think? Would you like to take a break?'

Then I followed a SMARTER plan with them both. Before finishing I asked them both if they need to say anything else to, or ask anything else of, each other. Then I closed the meeting. Endings are important. I thanked both boys for their commitment to working things through and for their courage and honesty. Following our meeting, both students shared that they were able to move forward and there had been no further conflict.

IT'S NOT A SCRIPT, IT'S JUST A STRUCTURE

The structure is very important as it provides a consistent approach to running restorative conferences, so everyone has the same opportunities. Over the years two different approaches to restorative conferences have been pioneered, and these are important to recognise. One is a scripted approach, such as the real justice script, originally developed by Terry O'Connell.[14] Others, like Tim Chapman in Northern Ireland[15] and Dominic Barter in Brazil,[16] do not use a scripted model; their approach is much more about dialogue.

We prefer to use a structure rather than a script. The important thing is that whoever is involved – students, staff and families – experiences a meeting that feels safe enough to allow them to talk through what's happened, explore the impact on each other, discuss any unmet needs and come up with a plan to prevent a reoccurrence. Of course, the individuals involved will have a bearing on how you go about the process and there is no equality in treating everyone equal. A certain amount of personalisation and adaptation is necessary to best meet the needs of the students and families you work with:

- Remember that engagement takes three forms: physical, emotional and mental. All three aspects need to be thought about in advance.

- You don't have to use the same questions in every situation. You might need to ask fewer, or more, questions at times. You might need to use visual aids or prompts to help children express themselves.

---

14 See T. O'Connell, *Conferencing Handbook: The New Real Justice Training Manual* (Pipersville, PA: The Piper's Press, 1998).
15 See, for example, A. Dzur, Conversations on Restorative Justice: A Talk with Tim Chapman, *Restorative Justice* 4(1) (2016): 115–129.
16 For more information, see: J. Wachtel, Toward Peace and Justice in Brazil: Dominic Barter and Restorative Circles, *IIRP News* (20 March 2009). Available at: https://www.iirp.edu/news/toward-peace-and-justice-in-brazil-dominic-barter-and-restorative-circles.

- Having a distraction can help while having a one-on-one conversation. Playing with building blocks, colouring in, etc. works – as might handling a stress ball for older students.

- If you're having a restorative chat with one student, it is often better to take a walk or be outside. Sitting side by side on low chairs can often be more productive than sitting in a formal room.

- If you're having a meeting with more people, give plenty of thought to the seating arrangement (for more on this, see Chapter 5). Will you sit in a circle? Where will you place yourself in the room? Who will you start with? Do you need a talking piece (i.e. an object, such as a ball or a furry dice, that is circulated between participants to hold in order to indicate that they 'have the floor' – much like the conch in *Lord of the Flies*)? And, of course, there's the question of tissues, drinks and custard creams – all helpful and necessary if dealing with heavy topics.

- The time of day needs to be carefully considered for all parties, taking into account work commitments, travel times and the likes if parents or careers are involved.

- And, don't forget, connect before content.

Does this take more time? Of course. But it is time in the bank and you will save it in the long run. After all, repeat offending needs repeat punishing. Get it right the first time and you'll get less in the way of repeat business. The trick is to get involved earlier in the life of the problem, earlier in the life of the child.

And the impact? Students become better at self-regulating and more confident problem-solvers. We would also hope that this in turn would ensure that students are more engaged in learning and are achieving more. When we work with and alongside young people, rather than make decisions about them in isolation, outcomes and impacts are so much better.

CHAPTER 4
RESTORATIVE CIRCLES

EVERYTHING LOOKS BETTER WHEN YOU PUT IT IN A CIRCLE[1]

So, something powerful starts to happen when we shift our language. But there is another tweak to the way we do things that can make a big difference to relationships: and it's as simple as routinely rearranging the furniture. I'm sure there is some law of the universe that states that any chairs left unattended in a school will always arrange themselves in straight lines. Either that or caretaker college doesn't even cover the possibility of anything other than rows and right angles. However, in a school that is genuinely embracing restorative practices, 'sit in circles, not lines of authority' has to be the motto.

Sitting in a circle of chairs means that everyone can see each other, there is no start and no end, and any sense of hierarchy is diminished (no one is sitting at the head of the table). It also means that, as there is no back row to a circle, everyone is encouraged to be involved – we're all crew and not passengers – and it's easier to communicate verbally and non-verbally.

Circles are an easy way to build connections and create a sense of belonging, and are the obvious space for seeking to repair harm and relationships. Indeed, they are a natural

---
1 Professor Gale Burford said this to me, and in turn attributed it to his circle of connections.

shape we use regularly in our lives, perhaps without even realising. When you meet friends in a pub or a café, do you prefer to have a round table so you can all see each other? When you go out for a meal in a group, large round tables are much more sociable than long thin ones, aren't they? The same goes for picnics – we end up sitting in a circle on the blanket. And, if you play sport, how often does the captain or coach gather everyone in a circle for a team talk? You get the message, but in schools, suggesting rearranging the furniture can be quite uncomfortable.

Of course, there can be limits on what we can arrange so, for example, sitting in a 'square-circle' can be OK (just watch out for hidden voices in the corners). Sitting on the carpet can work, as can standing up (especially if you want it to be a quick meeting). The important thing is that we can all see each other, and we are all in the same space – one without hierarchy in which everyone can feel equal. Circles are the geometric shape for community.

Circles need to become the way things are done round here. As we'll see in Chapter 5, circles are the ideal form for restorative meetings. However, if, like cowboys in the Wild West, the only time you 'circle up' is when there's trouble, then the automatic response to circles will soon be one of resistance, defensiveness and negativity. And not just by the children. Ensure circles are integrated into your week and don't allow them to become the first thing that's dropped when you get busy, as this will devalue their use.

Equally, do not be afraid to add to the weekly tally of circle opportunities as the need arises and you become more confident with their effectiveness and application. For example, I have seen them used well after lunch, when classes are struggling to settle, to celebrate successes, to alter the learning environment or to discuss and agree new ways of working together. So, in this chapter, we'll explore how to integrate restorative circles into your classroom, and discuss some of their uses.

I worked with a primary school in Yorkshire who made the decision to use a check-in and a check-out circle each day: every morning and at the end of every day. This gave each class an opportunity to check in with each other, to make sure that every child was acknowledged, to say good morning and for each child and adult to exchange deposits in their relationship banks. The aim was to build community.

One secondary school I worked with in Greater Manchester decided to redesign tutor times on Monday and Friday mornings to focus on nothing other than relationships in form groups. On Monday morning they would discuss highlights from the weekend (always with boundaries), and how everyone is feeling (on a scale of 1 to 10) that morning. If our students give themselves a low score, it gives us an opportunity to follow up and try to understand what's happening for that child and how we can support them. Getting involved earlier in the life of a problem always helps. The questions you ask are always built on what you are trying to achieve and what your desired outcome is.

A primary school I worked with decided to use check-in circles on a Monday morning for five to ten minutes to start to build connections between all staff. They decided to do a simple go-around-the-circle asking questions that would help everyone get to know each other further. A colleague who was new to the school commented a month or so in how well she felt connected to all staff. When I unpicked it with her she felt she would have connected with colleagues in Key Stage 2 (where she worked and that part of the school), but might have gone days without getting to know office staff, Key Stage 1, etc. if it wasn't for the circles. If you serious about relationships, you have to be serious about creating relationship-building and relationship-maintaining opportunities. Don't forget, relationships aren't built in a day; they are built daily.

SOLUTION-FOCUSED CIRCLES

Do you ever get stuck with a problem, and question what to do next? Do students come to you seeking solutions to their problems? How often do we spend large amounts of time on problems and much less time on solutions? How often do we focus on the past to the extent that we do not have the chance to design the future? Well, there is a very simple five-step process that you can use to help by utilising the support of the people around you. I even know of a school that holds these gatherings at lunchtime with the children running them.

In a solution-focused circle, the person with the issue has the full support of the other members of the circle. They will be heard, in a non-judgemental way, and assisted to find ways to progress the issue. The important thing is to spend less time on the problem and more time on the solutions.

THE PROCESS

Solution-focused circles, action learning and peer supervision models have been around for years and this process gives a nod to those practices. The following five steps to success have been refined with, and alongside, too many colleagues to name over a number of years.

Before you begin, arrange the chairs in a circle so that everyone can see each other.

STAGE 1 – THE ISSUE

The issue to be dealt with is clearly outlined by the person without any interruption from the group. Allow up to two minutes for this; it should not take any longer than that. Outlining what the primary concern is and how the person is stuck helps the group to be ready to ask the right clarification questions in stage 2.

STAGE 2 – CLARIFICATION QUESTIONS

This is the only stage when there is dialogue between the group and the person with the issue. The group is encouraged to ask clarification questions, typically, 'When does this …?', 'How often will they …?', 'Who is involved?', etc.

At this stage it is critical that no solutions are offered. Nor should there be any enquiries about ideas, solutions and interventions that may have been tried before. We do not want to establish a dialogue of 'I've tried that and it didn't work!' This will choke off suggestions for solutions and stop the creative flow. What we are seeking to achieve is to draw on the collective brain of the group and allow group members to spark ideas off each other. To this end, only clarification questions may be asked, ones that are not judgemental or critical.

STAGE 3 – SOLUTIONS

This stage of the process requires the person with the issue to write down the solutions and possible ways forward offered by the other members of the circle. They must take care not to respond to any of the suggestions, even if they have been tried before. They must just listen and note the suggestions down.

STAGE 4 – SELECTION

The subject of the process will reflect and then select the two suggestions that they will action and use in the future. They share these with the group so that the group can check in with them at a future date to ensure that they have been actioned.

STAGE 5 – SUPPORT

This is where we can ask for support from within the group to achieve the specific goals that have been selected in stage 4.

It is important for someone to facilitate the process to enable the clear demarcation of the separate steps and to stop them blurring into each other. The timings are up to you, but the four stages are essential. Typically, there will be less time given to outline the issue and more time for solutions. I usually allow two minutes for stage 1, four minutes for stage 2 and four minutes for stage 3. The timing of stage 4 is up to the person with the issue as it's their job to reflect on the solutions. I've also trained children to use this structure – for example, for resolving issues in the playground – and they typically use shorter times. Depending on the issue, 10–20 seconds might be long enough to outline the problem, then 30 seconds for clarifying questions and 30 seconds for suggestions.

THE CARR MANOR WAY (PART 1)

Carr Manor Community School for students aged 4–19 serves one of the most diverse catchment areas in Leeds, including communities facing significant deprivation. The school's leadership team were aware that they needed to improve outcomes for some of the most vulnerable children and those with the most complex needs and that what they were doing just simply wasn't up to the job. In the spring of 2012 they decided to take a different, more holistic, approach and began work to improve attendance and reduce exclusions by using restorative practices in all aspects of school life.

On a Monday, classes begin slightly later than the rest of the week. Monday mornings are important. They set the tone. Weather is created on a Monday. First, the leadership team will sit in a circle and check in with each other – how was your weekend? What are the highlights for you for the week ahead? What challenges are you facing this week? After that, in the school hall, whole-staff coaching takes place, with staff members sitting in their coaching group circles to have their turn to 'check in' for the week ahead. It is a time for staff training and for thinking about the students and the school's focus for the week ahead.

'We find that having that time to meet each other, speak to each other and above all listen to each other and have our own voices heard, is very powerful and brings the organisation to a very good place by 9.00am every Monday,' says Simon Flowers, the school's executive principal.

When the students arrive, they go into their coaching groups of seven to ten children, cross-phase (the school is an all-through school), each with an adult coach and some with assistant coaches too. Then it's their turn to check in, with the coaches leading a discussion that focuses on the weekend and the week ahead for half an hour. What's more, this process is also repeated mid-week as a 'check-up' and on Friday afternoons as a 'check-out', ready for the weekend.

In the words of the school's executive principal:

> *'We find that having an established and structured process like this helps to build a culture where everyone has a voice, and everyone is listened to. Undertaking coaching circles three times a week creates an ongoing dialogue and a community of trust where everyone – staff member or pupil – knows that their concerns and contributions will be heard. It also allows us to share information rapidly across a school community of around 1,650 people (staff and pupils), which is a great advantage.'*

Rather than use restorative practice as a response to negative incidents (more justice than practice), they have adopted a whole-school approach in which restorative behaviour is at the core of everything they do (we'll find out more about this in Chapter 6).

CHECK-IN AND CHECK-OUT CIRCLES

Checking in with our students and our classes is so important. The biggest thing we can learn is that we matter to others. Being valued can help us feel safe and secure. Check-in and check-out circles are fundamental to forming strong relationships and so are crucial in building a strong sense of community. They are also key to knowing our children well and allowing them to know us well.

In primary schools, you might check in and out as a class, or split the class into two groups, as smaller circles are slightly easier to manage. In secondary, you might check in and out as a tutor group or we might be courageous enough to create small mixed-age groups that meet on Monday mornings to check in for the week ahead and on Friday mornings to check out at the end of the week. You might even decide to hold a 'check-up' midweek to see how things are going. Carr Manor Community School follows this approach. Groups consisting of approximately ten students gathered from all year groups meet three times a week in timetabled sessions: Monday morning, Wednesday afternoon and Friday morning. On Fridays, students can celebrate their successes from the week and also share their plans for the weekend with the rest of the group.

Creating these spaces across the week sets firm expectations and offers the support and nurture students need to get there. At Carr Manor, the success of this approach was evidenced in their last Ofsted report, which stated that:

> *The school's coaching programme is a major strength of the school. The impact of this programme on relationships between staff and pupils and the inclusive ethos of the school are impressive.*[2]

If we dedicated time to ensuring that we 'just' strengthened relationships, would it be enough? Surely social and emotional needs and growth are just as important as academic growth? It's important that circles fit our classroom needs; we need to use them to create a classroom culture in which students feel safe, supported and ready to learn.

Surely we can find five – or even up to 20 – minutes to check in? The Monday check-in circle works with students,

---

2 Ofsted, Short Inspection: Carr Manor Community School, Specialist Sports College (26 June 2018), p. 2. Available at: https://files.ofsted.govuk/v1/file/2786537.

and with colleagues, and is a great way to set yourself up for the week ahead. We could use the following routine at the start of the week:

- Greeting: students and teachers greet and welcome each other.

- Sharing: students share something about themselves or their lives, their peers listen and then ask follow-up questions or offer comments. Teachers also offer something of their personal self. Remember, we don't want anyone to share anything private, just little parts of themselves as investments in the social capital bank.

- Activity: the group completes an activity that encourages collaboration and community building.

- Communication: sharing of any team, class or whole-school messages.

The goal is to establish connections, deepen relationships, build a sense of community, and create the conditions in which trust can be built, in which there are opportunities for empathy and collaboration is encouraged. Check-in circles work because they are done in every classroom every week. They are not optional. It's not a question of 'If there's time'. They are not for some staff but not others. They are for everyone, always. That is how you build such practices into the culture of the school. At the heart is the idea that, if we want our children to have a voice, the whole community needs to be willing to listen and taught how.

As ever, being consistent needs to be matched with being flexible and responsive to circumstances, and the approach needs to be age-appropriate. For example, with younger children, you might share high fives or smiles, rather than going through the whole process, and it might take a few minutes, rather than 15–20. Or, to start with, rather than working with the whole class, you might group the students into two or even three smaller circles.

COMMUNICATING IN CIRCLES

When it comes to establishing a group's ability to listen to others and take turns, sometimes the proverbial conch can help: something that symbolises whose turn it is to talk. Apart from developing their listening skills – a key social skill – this process can also really help students to develop their speaking ability. Having an audience genuinely listen to you is a great way to make what you have to say feel meaningful and worthwhile. And this is all the more true for those quieter students.

The key to great circle conversations is the quality of the questions being asked. The questions you ask will depend on what you are trying to achieve. It's about thinking through your questions, how long you have available, how old the students are, and their needs and circumstances. We need to understand our students, understand class dynamics and create a safe environment. We can also use questioning effectively by linking it to student and school priorities.

Crafting the right question will help you achieve your desired outcome. They are also great at getting conversations going. A good question prompts a good conversation. The right question invites students and staff into the circle and asks them to share a little part of themselves. Do remember the difference between the personal and private, though.

Questions can be simple and light-hearted, they can be more personal or more professional (asking about outside or inside school), they can be about experiences or imagination, they explore our feelings and what's happening to us and they can ask about complex and important issues.

A few examples to get you started might be:

- What's your favourite sport?
- If you could have one superpower, what would you choose?
- What's your favourite food?
- What's your favourite season when it comes to the weather?
- What's your favourite TV show or book?
- What's your favourite colour?
- If you could be an animal for the day, which animal would you be?
- What's your favourite lesson?
- What's one thing that you enjoyed over the weekend?
- If you were the prime minister or the president for the day, what would you do?
- What's one thing that's made you feel proud today?
- If you were in charge of the school for a day, what would you do?
- If you had a day off school, what would you do and where would you go?
- What do you like to collect?
- What is your passion?
- What gives you hope?

- If you could make a change in your community, what change would you make?

Don't forget to carefully select the question for the situation. The well-being and safeguarding of all is most important. Be sensitive and know your class well. Be prepared and know that some circle questions may bring up emotions. Most of all, the question must help you to achieve your, and the class', desired outcome.

PREPARING FOR CIRCLES TO SUCCEED

Successful circles don't just happen. In the beginning, children will need time to adjust, to get used to them and see how they work. People need time to relax, engage with one another and build trust little by little. It will feel easier to chime in when having more challenging conversations if the atmosphere is right, so we need to spend time establishing norms and expectations – what I call 'circle norms' – and teaching the behaviours that will help the sessions to go as smoothly as possible. These must be revisited regularly throughout the year and refined to meet the needs and abilities of the participants.

Establish the group norms at the first session. Your first group circle activity should be all about identifying clearly how that group will work together, what they expect from each other and how they should relate to each other when working in this way. An example of such norms could include a no inappropriate laughter rule. You'll also need to establish the importance of confidentiality, the need for no side-talking, the manner in which anyone can contribute or is allowed to pass, and the importance of speaking from the heart. It might also be beneficial to set boundaries about what things of a personal nature should and should not be discussed (and, with safeguarding in mind, where to take personal issues).

One critical rule is that everyone present in the room should be taking part and positioned in the circle. There should be nothing distracting going on outside the circle. This is true whether you're in the classroom or the staffroom. I have seen examples of poor meeting practice, for example, in which teaching assistants sat outside the circle getting on with some preparation work. Apart from being an unnecessary distraction, this really misses the point of community building: the expectation that everyone should be present and contributing.

How will you rearrange your classroom so that the seats can be moved into a circle? One school I worked with placed stickers on the floor so that children knew where to place their table and chairs. In another the children had until the end of a specific song to move the furniture into place. Another had a carpet area where circles would take place. Where you sit is important, as is who you sit with. Some teachers encourage children to sit next to someone other than their best friend, but that's up to you as a class to decide. There are plenty of books out there with fun games that you can use as mixers. Jenny Mosley's circle time resources are familiar to schools and are great to give structure, exercises and parts of social and emotional aspects of learning.[3] *The Little Book of Thunks* by Ian Gilbert[4] and *The Complete Book of Questions* by Garry Poole[5] can be great places to start. Of course, sometimes

---

[3] See https://www.circle-time.co.uk/.
[4] I. Gilbert, *The Little Book of Thunks: 260 Questions to Make Your Brain Go Ouch!* (Carmarthen: Independent Thinking Press, 2007).
[5] G. Poole, *The Complete Book of Questions: 1001 Conversation Starters for Any Occasion* (Grand Rapids, MI: Zondervan, 2003).

it's better for children to sit with peers or adults who help them to feel safe.

So, you can't expect students, or staff, to start opening up and participating overnight. Even the most communicative groups need some warm-up, and all groups will need to be introduced to whatever rules and guidelines you feel are necessary to make the circle successful. By agreeing the rules *with* (that word again) the group, you build ownership and responsibility, and thus allow them to respectfully challenge each other and you.

CHAPTER 5
RESTORATIVE MEETINGS AND CONFERENCES

SETTING MEETINGS UP TO SUCCEED

A restorative – or indeed any important – meeting is one that works intentionally and deliberately to create a safe space in which to discuss difficult or sensitive issues with the purpose of improving relationships, resolving conflict and easing tensions between people. That's the same whether the meeting is addressing issues that are student-to-student, staff-to-student, or staff-to-staff. Three words sum up the best restorative meetings: preparation, preparation, preparation. Why would you not set them up to succeed?

I've heard some horror stories over the years about so-called restorative meetings that have done more harm than good due to poor handling or lack of the necessary care and understanding, especially if either party has been forced to participate against their will. Having someone sit across the circle from an individual who has harmed them in some way is a highly sensitive situation and needs to be handled with great care. Of course, a restorative meeting doesn't have to be about harm; it can also be about relationship breakdowns and tensions between members of the school community. A restorative meeting is first and foremost about respect. Making people participate isn't respectful and it is not good practice.

Addressing small low-level disruptions or breakdowns in community life might not need as much preparation and, indeed, the process might be quite short once the groundwork has been laid and we all know how we behave in a restorative school. When matters are of a more serious nature, we really must think about what needs to be in place beforehand to ensure that the meeting will succeed. It must be safe and well-focused, and have the right students, staff and/or families in attendance.

Such meetings, by their conflict-born nature, bring with them an element of risk, but if you don't seek to resolve the conflict, it will only spill over into the rest of the school day. Now's your chance to nip that in the bud. If you fail to act out of fear of risk, you miss a great opportunity to help all those concerned.

Here is my checklist of things to consider when it comes to setting up a restorative meeting to succeed:

- First and foremost, decide who is the best person to facilitate the meeting. It's not enough to just ask someone who is available at the time. Can they be seen as neutral? Do they have ample time to conduct the meeting?
- Meet with the parties separately before the meeting to explore what happened from their perspective. What were their thoughts, feelings and attitudes at the time of the incident and what are they now?
- Establish their expectations of the process.
- Ask about their motivation for being involved. What outcome or outcomes would they like to see?

- Are there any communication difficulties to consider – for example, from an English as an additional language (EAL) or special educational needs and disabilities (SEND) perspective – and, if so, how can we adapt the process accordingly? The important thing is to know your students well so you know what needs to be done to make the meeting inclusive.

- Has there been, or is there likely to be, any intimidation of any of the participants and is it safe to go ahead with the meeting?

- Is there any previous history between the participants that might have impacted on this incident?

- Are there any constraints on the location and time for the restorative meeting?

- What support might need to be given before, during or by way of follow-up?

- Take time to explore the ground rules and expectations before the meeting. What does everyone need in order for the meeting to go well?

With regard to timings, best practice says there should be no time constraints but, in a busy school, that might not be entirely practical, so make sure everyone is clear. 'We have this amount of time and we must do X, Y and Z within that time frame.'

Of course, there are other practical aspects to consider, such as where the meeting will take place, who needs to be there and who definitely shouldn't be there. Do you need a break-out space for more sensitive meetings in case anyone needs a time out? Do you have plenty of tissues to hand in case anyone gets upset? What refreshments will you provide? You'd be amazed at how different a meeting can feel when you have a cup of tea in your hand. And as for the restorative power of the custard cream …

Something else to consider is the removal of barriers, and not just emotional ones. If the meeting involves parents, carers and important others, does the meeting need to be held off-site to increase engagement? Sadly, lots of parents struggle to come into school. Is the meeting at a convenient time and are there any other barriers to their attendance? Other considerations include how they will arrive. If inviting in families or people from the wider community, are they all likely to be walking into the school reception – or whichever chosen space – at the same time, and is that advisable?

As mentioned, connecting with the participants before the meeting either face-to-face or by telephone (or Zoom) is important. During this pre-meeting discussion you can introduce the sorts of restorative questions that will be used. This gives everyone time to prepare their thoughts and responses, which will make for a more productive meeting all round. How often do we allow no preparation time and then act surprised when we ask questions and the answer is 'I don't know'? It is important to explore the participants' needs – not their wants – in terms of the outcomes they would like to see from the meeting, so you can ask them to start thinking about this in advance.

SETTING UP THE SEATS

As anyone who has planned a wedding reception knows full well, the seating plan is the part of the planning process that is most fraught with danger. Deciding who should sit next to whom – and who should be kept as far apart as possible – is important for all concerned, and has made or broken many an event, restorative or otherwise. It is important, therefore, to consider who will sit where, especially in more sensitive meetings. Of course, having supporters in the best place for a child can be enormously beneficial too. Being surrounded by people who love and care for you can really help in important meetings.

We've seen how everything looks better in a circle but, of course, other variations on a theme exist. The main thing is that I don't want to be sitting behind a desk for a restorative chat, nor do I want to be sitting directly opposite anyone as that might feel confrontational. Instead, I choose to arrange the seats side-by-side and at an angle, so we can sit next to each other to look at problems and solutions. I might ignore the seats and kneel down or sit on the floor next to younger children. If two students are in conflict and we are bringing them together, I might choose to set the seats out in a V-shape: me at the bottom and the two students at the top.

But don't forget that engagement takes three forms: physical, mental and emotional. It's not just about the physical space; it's about how we create the conditions for mental and emotional engagement. The removal of threat is not the same as the creation of safety. Arranging the room means taking into account the physical, mental and emotional needs of all concerned to ensure the meeting's best chance for success. You are not simply organising logistics but also power, ensuring that it is shared evenly through countless little things. We must bear in mind the question, 'What would help everyone to feel safe and engaged in this meeting?' It's all about those 1% marginal gains.

RUNNING A MORE FORMAL RESTORATIVE CONFERENCE

Sometimes, restorative chats and informal meetings aren't enough and we need to bring out the big guns, so to speak. No matter how good we are at relational working as a school, the scale and complexity of the issue at hand might need us to take things to another level – a restorative conference, as it is often called. Be assured, though, that despite the seriousness of the circumstances we can still work towards a resolution without losing our restorative vision.

A restorative conference is a planned face-to-face meeting in which a trained (neutral and impartial – in short, not involved) facilitator brings together those who've been harmed, and anyone else who has been affected, in order to explore what's happened, the impact that it's had on everyone, what their needs are and what needs to happen to move forward. I'd like to recognise the work of the Australian theorist John Braithwaite,[1] Australian trainer John McDonald[2] and police officer Terry O'Connell,[3] whose work has helped develop and then spread the idea and practice of restorative conferencing around the world.

There are a number of other restorative conference models available, but some common elements are as follows:

- One-to-one facilitative preparation discussions should be held with all involved parties prior to the event to

---

1 See http://johnbraithwaite.com/about/.
2 See https://proactive-resolutions.com/.
3 See, for example, T. O'Connell, *Restorative Justice for Police: Foundations for Change*. Paper presented at the United Nations Crime Congress, Ancillary Meeting on Implementing Restorative Justice in the International Context. Vienna, Austria (10-17 April 2000). Available at: http://restorativejustice.org/10fulltext/oconnell.

discuss what a restorative conference is, how it works and whether they agree to take part.

- Scheduling the conference at a time that suits all.
- Seating all participants in a circle in a neutral space in a venue that works for all.
- Introducing all participants by the name they prefer.
- Opening the discussion by asking the person who caused the harm to describe what happened and the impact it had on them and others from their perspective.
- Inviting the person harmed and then all other participants to describe what happened and the impact it had on them and others from their perspective.
- When everyone has shared their perspective, all participants are invited to suggest how the harm might be repaired with the aim of reaching an agreement.
- If a written plan is needed, this is pulled together and written up by the facilitator and shared with everyone involved.

This might sound similar to what we would do with restorative conversations; however, the difference here is that the meetings are more formal and potentially more sensitive, so the preparation needs to be too. Preparation for a restorative conversation might take a few minutes; for a more formal restorative conference, the preparation could take a few hours or even longer.

STEPS TO SUCCESS

Restorative approaches work because they are never seen in isolation: there is always a before, a during and an after. Restorative conferences are no different and should be thought of in terms of three important phases:

1 Preparation.

2 The conference itself.

3 Post-conference support and monitoring.

During the preparation phase, a trained and neutral facilitator will agree to work with students, staff and the family involved to develop an understanding of what's happened before the official meeting. This gives the facilitator the opportunity to get to know everyone, to identify and discuss any specific needs and to agree the purpose and focus of the conference.

During the conference, the person who did the deed begins by telling their side of the story from their perspective. This is followed by the person who has been affected doing likewise. Both then have a chance to express their feelings about the events and circumstances, followed by anyone else who has been affected doing the same.

Under the careful and watchful eye of the trained facilitator, the offender and the offended may then direct questions at one another, followed by questions posed by their respective families or supporters. The offender and their family will then meet privately to discuss what reparation they feel is in order and will return to present an offer to the victim. If this is not accepted, then negotiations will continue until a genuine consensus is reached. The agreement is put in writing, if needed, with a clear plan. Post-conference, the facilitator monitors completion of the agreement and helps the group locate any required resources.

It is important to offer monitoring and ongoing support, for example:

- Assist with and monitor the completion of the agreement (if there is one, as the meeting – through dialogue, understanding, apologies, etc. – might have been enough in itself).

- Staff, families and other students can assist the student in completing their outcome agreement.

- If the student has not completed the agreement, assess whether any further support you could give would enable them to do so.

- If further support is impossible or ineffective, sensitively inform those who were affected and, if needed, convene another meeting with careful and sensitive preparation to avoid the risk of revictimising them.

- If an individual has not delivered on the agreement, ensure that structures are put in place to pass this information back to the appropriate tutor, head of year, senior leader and parents or carers to explore further.

A FIVE-STEP PROCESS FOR FACILITATING A RESTORATIVE CONFERENCE

A trained, neutral facilitator is absolutely critical to the success of any restorative conference. Here is a five-step process for facilitating a restorative conference once everyone is in the room, settled and sitting in the circle.

STEP 1 – INTRODUCTIONS AND SETTING THE FOCUS

- Welcome everyone and do a round of introductions.
- Explore and agree what everyone needs from each other for the meeting to go well. What are the ground rules, group norms and expectations of each other? The removal of threat is not the same as the creation of safety.
- Set the focus for the meeting and establish what it is that has brought everyone together.
- Conduct any necessary housekeeping.
- Offer a brief reminder about the process and the role of the facilitator.

STEP 2 – THE STORYTELLING PHASE

- Ask everyone, one at a time, the following restorative questions in turn:
    - What happened (before and after)?

- What were your thoughts and feelings (before and after)?
- Who has been affected and how (impact)?

- The key is understanding that everyone might have a different perspective on what has happened and that's OK. Remember the three truths.

- Reiterate that this is an opportunity for everyone to have their say – and be listened to. It's important to keep bringing everyone back to the agreement they made at the beginning about what they need from each other. Safety throughout the process is crucial.

STEP 3 – THE REFLECTION PHASE

- Ask everyone: 'Can you see the impact X has had on Y and Z?'

- If they can't see the impact, then you have moved on from step 2 too quickly and need to backtrack. If they are nodding and saying that they can, then the impact needs to be explored fully before moving on to the next question.

- The next question is also for everyone: 'Are you ready to think about what needs to happen next?' At this stage, we are not looking for everyone to come up with a plan. We are just looking to reach the consensus that they are ready to move on.

STEP 4 – THE AGREEMENT PHASE

- Ask everyone: 'What needs do you have and how can they be met?' Or 'What needs to happen for things to move forward?'

- Explore with everyone, in a *with* way, a plan that they can all agree to and, importantly, that meets everyone's needs.
- Check with each individual what they need and what they are going to do – form a plan.
- Ensure your goals are SMARTER.

STEP 5 – SUMMING UP AND CLOSING THE MEETING

- Summarise the plan by reflecting it back to the group and making sure everyone is happy with it. Does anything need tweaking or changing? Is the plan achievable and realistic?
- Ask if they need to meet again, to check how things are going and, if so, when and where. This needs to be led by the group.
- Ask the group: 'Is there anything else you need from each other or anything further that you would like to add?' It's important that nobody leaves the meeting with unmet needs or feels that they have not had their say or were not listened to.
- Thank everyone for taking part and for their contributions and commitments. How we end the meeting, and how students and staff feel, is as important as how we greet them. Conflict not properly transformed will only ever end up being transferred.

CONFLICT AS PROPERTY

We have to organise our relational systems so that conflicts are nurtured and made visible and see to it that professionals do not monopolise the handling of them. If we aren't careful, student-to-student, student-to-staff or staff-to-staff conflicts are taken away, given away or are made invisible. But does it really matter?

In 1977, Norwegian sociologist and criminologist Nils Christie wrote an important article relating to restorative justice entitled Conflicts as Property.[4] I was lucky enough to see the man himself speak at the University of Hull in 2010 as part of a small event organised by the law and criminology department and heard what he had to say first-hand. The idea of conflict as property has always given me much food for thought and I understand it now to be a crucial element of thinking in a restorative way about conflict and about repairing the harm to relationships which that conflict has caused.

In a nutshell, Christie argued that:

> *My suspicion is that criminology to some extent has amplified a process where conflicts have been taken away from the parties directly involved and thereby have either disappeared or become other people's property.*[5]

In other words, the victim and the perpetrator lose ownership of the event as the contravention of the system's rules takes precedence over the human actors involved. Or, put even more simply, it's a missed opportunity.

In a school setting, if we aren't careful, by focusing on which school rule was broken and what the rule book says

---

4   N. Christie, Conflicts as Property, *The British Journal of Criminology* 17(1) (1977): 1-15. Available at: https://academic.oup.com/bjc/article/17/1/1/411623.

5   Christie, Conflicts as Property, 1.

should be the punishment, we leave our students and staff out of the dialogue and decision making. The conflict has become school property. In this way, the victim has no chance, ever, to come to know more about the perpetrator. They are left outside – physically and metaphorically – feeling angry, hurt and possibly humiliated, without contact with the perpetrator and without participation in a discussion of how they could repair the damage. What's more, the perpetrator will never *fully* know the effects of their actions. They lose the opportunity to explain themselves. They lose the opportunity to put things right. They also lose one of the most important possibilities – that of being forgiven.

In restorative schools, children are encouraged to solve issues themselves, to take ownership of and responsibility for what needs to happen next. To achieve this, we need to be in the *with* box with them, modelling great questions and possibility thinking. A focus on sanction and blame results in an adversarial, punish-to-deter experience, by which no deeper lessons are really learned, those affected are often ignored and accountability is never fully experienced. With a more question-led restorative approach, the focus is on repairing harm and addressing accountability, while putting things right for the sake of each other rather than the sake of the system.

If we accept the premise that conflict is a natural part of any worthwhile relationship, then our focus isn't on avoiding the possibility of strong disagreements ever happening but on using dialogue to seek to understand and grow. If children compliantly behave simply because it's what they've been told to do, they are missing out on an opportunity to develop as rational, connected and emotionally mature young adults. 'Because I say so' and the fear of punishment is no replacement for a deeper understanding of how to be with and act towards others.

Christie argues – and my experience tells me that – a student's full participation in their own conflict is more important than any automated cause-and-effect, crime-and-punishment scenario. After all, conflict is healthy; what we do with it often isn't. Doing harm, learning how to come to terms with our effect on others and how to repair our relationships is the very stuff of learning to be a responsible citizen. Every appropriation of this learning by the system is a missed opportunity to affect real behavioural change. After all, as everyone's favourite head teacher Vic Goddard wrote:

> *Exclusions don't work. If they did, we would only ever exclude a student once.*[6]

---

[6] Goddard, *The Best Job in the World*, p. 152.

CHAPTER 6

PRACTICE SUSTAINABILITY

ONE SIZE DOESN'T FIT ALL; IN FACT, IT ONLY EVER FITS ONE

So, where do you begin as a school if you think you would like to embrace a restorative approach? Here are some quick pointers to help you think about what should happen next. As with any new ideas, an approach cannot succeed unless senior leaders understand – and, more importantly, believe in – what they are trying to do, and it aligns with the vision and ethos of the school.

Meetings and short introductory sessions are good starting points for covering the basics of restorative practice. The aim is to help everyone see and understand that this approach is ultimately best for the school community. As part of this process, a school should assess its readiness for implementation before embarking on change. This is done through conversations and listening to staff members, students and families.

If you are a member of the leadership team, you might find this simple list helpful:

- Consider your why and your how.
- Have a vision for what you want to achieve and develop a plan accordingly.
- Make sure it is owned and understood by all.

- Restorative practice is not a one-off event; it's part of a bigger strategy.
- Create the conditions for your plan to be successful.
- If restorative practice is the main thing, keep it the main thing.
- Assess where you are now and be brutally honest – confront the facts.
- Involve students and families at every stage.
- Develop an implementation plan with clear priorities and an outcomes framework.
- Develop a clear vision of what it will look like when it's working well.
- Consider what behaviours you expect to see.
- Make use of internal evaluations.
- Use qualitative feedback, narratives and stories. Don't underestimate the stories.
- Create short-term wins and communicate them.
- Use external research partners.
- Bring all your evaluations into one place.
- Be courageous!

I hope these points get you started – on your thinking, at the very least.

Since 2006 I have used John Kotter's eight steps for leading change as a structure to help implement restorative practice successfully.[1] I would highly recommend that you check out his work, particularly his book *Our Iceberg Is*

---

1 See https://www.kotterinc.com/8-steps-process-for-leading-change/.

Melting.[2] I would also recommend the book *Who Moved My Cheese?* by Dr Spencer Johnson.[3]

It is so important that school leaders communicate to staff that 'restorative practices are going to be the way we do things around here'. In other words, the decision has been made and how we make it reality is now down to us all. As with any whole-school change, in order to be successful with restorative practices, there needs to be a critical mass of staff who actively support and engage in this approach. It may be hard to gauge staff buy-in before implementation has begun; however, school leadership should (using the power of *with*) involve staff, students and families early in the development stages to assess willingness. A level of trust needs to be developed across the staff, as any new approach requires us to be vulnerable, open and ready to ask for help when we need it.

PLANTING THE SEEDS OF CHANGE

The seeds of successful change must be planted by embedding procedural and behavioural changes in an organisation before the launch of any new initiative. Sometimes an initiative calls for sweeping changes in the school's processes, systems and culture. The launch proceeds with great fanfare (bacon barms (breadcakes in Yorkshire), even bowls of posh chocolates on the tables and everything) and a substantial investment of the

---

2 J. Kotter and H. Rathgeber, *Our Iceberg Is Melting: Changing and Succeeding Under Any Conditions* (London: Macmillan, 2006).

3 S. Johnson, *Who Moved My Cheese? An Amazing Way to Deal with Change in Your Work and in Your Life* (London: Vermilion, 1999).

school's resources. Several years later, however, leaders look back and wonder what went wrong.

Just as farmers prepare the land before their seeds are planted, so must we. When it comes to starting your own transformational change process – in no particular order and certainly not a complete list – here are some things that you'd do well to remember:

- Understand the current.
- Work through the approach upfront and map out the change process in detail.
- Be aware of the readiness for change and timings.
- There are no shortcuts to engaging and involving staff.
- Build an emotional case for change. Leaders can excel at convincing the head, but the heart must follow. Emotion can often create motion.
- Fit the changes into your wider strategic planning.
- Keep your eye on the real goal: the children.
- Leaders' behaviours have the greatest impact on an organisation's culture.
- Leaders must model the change – be the change, model the model, wear the t-shirt.
- Practise new behaviours together.
- Secure the time and resources required to implement the change process and see it through.
- Shake people out of their silos and comfort zones.
- Be clearly focused on the short- and long-term vision, but make sure there are some quick wins which are clearly communicated – and then over communicated – to all staff.

- Maintain the wins.
- Resist the urge to tweak until you are an expert.
- Communication strategies leading up to any kind of transformation are key and should be many, varied and often.
- Constantly check in and communicate using a variety of formal and informal methods to create a two-way street of dialogue and exchange.
- Maintain confidence in the face of setbacks or negative feedback.
- Create a feedback loop.
- Identify the big milestones – and party hard when you reach them.

For me, training in any new way of working, any behaviour model, any culture change, skill or tactic to make things better often falls down. Even if the training is great, everyone loves the ideas – hey, they even had fun – the risk is that they come back to a full timetable, back-to-back meetings and a million emails, and that's it. The trick is to focus on making change stick.

MAKING CHANGE STICK

People are the hardest part of change. Schools and organisations spend large sums of money and time on the external aspects of change programmes and, in my opinion, not enough on the internal side of change: inside the school, in your people, is where you really need to succeed in embedding new mindsets, practices and behaviours. Few of us have escaped the need for change in our careers; some of us relish the challenge and many of us have been involved in far too many changes, sadly, that are often more about grabbing headlines than hearts and minds. Regardless of how we feel about change and the frequency with which we are confronted with it, it's a tricky thing to make happen in an organisation – and that's something that doesn't change.

If we accept as eternal truths (1) that any change programme is a people process and (2) that humans are creatures of habit – prone to superhuman feats of resistance when it comes to adopting new systems, behaviours and practices – then we understand the way in which any change process is best approached. To put it simply, to achieve and sustain transformational change, we must capture the hearts and minds of everyone involved. The good news is that it can be done, as we can see in the example of Carr Manor.

THE CARR MANOR WAY (PART II)

Rather than simply use restorative practice as a response to negative incidents, Carr Manor has adopted a whole-school approach, where restorative behaviour is at the core of everything they do. Getting staff and student training right was where it all started, as school principal Simon Flowers told me, 'First we trained the staff in restorative practices and then the children, which enabled effective discussions where challenge and support are there in equal measure. In doing so, we've created a common language that enables us to resolve situations rapidly'.

The training of the children has been especially instrumental in creating a restorative approach to issues around conflict and behaviour. 'Over 250 children are trained as restorative practice representatives,' Simon continued, 'and are able to take responsibility for finding solutions and resolving conflicts. These pupils are trusted to take a conflict between others outside the classroom, resolve it, and go back in with a minimum of disruption to other pupils. They can also do this at other unstructured times during the day. The representatives are able to find solutions while issues might be smaller and easier to deal with, rather than allowing problems to escalate.'

Imagine how much staff time is freed up for other things with the children in this innovative 4–19 school self- and peer-regulating in this way.

Visitors to the school comment frequently on how calm and well behaved the students are, which Simon attributes in part to the restorative structure of the school. Statistics gathered since this way of working together was established are compelling:

'Our attendance has risen by 3.5 per cent to around 94 per cent, and remains high, which for a school with this range of complex needs is very hard to achieve,' Simon said. 'Fixed-term exclusions have fallen from 162 in the 2011/12 school year, to 12 in 2018/19 (three up to March 2019/20), which is a remarkable difference and has impacted significantly on the children and their outcomes.'

For Simon, however, statistics represent only part of the reason why restorative approaches have been so beneficial to the school. He said, 'I consider the main differences from before we started working in this way to be far less tangible. It's really about the relationships within the school, and how everyone talks and connects with each other, and supports and challenges each other.'

He continued, 'Schools are under constant pressure to improve a range of outcomes and there is a temptation to work in a way that isn't very restorative and to feel justified in doing so. So, schools can and do use processes and systems where the work is done "to" the children, whereas we work to the ideal that we want children to "choose to and want to", rather than "have to" because they're told to.'

Carr Manor's restorative approach is not limited to staff and students – parents and carers are also actively involved and have been effectively supported to work in this way. Simon said, 'It is so embedded that we can usually resolve difficulties very easily because everyone – parent, carer, child or teacher – is working in the same way towards a resolution that we're all happy with. When we have had conflict in the past we would have sent a pupil home. However, we now have trained staff to be able to arrange a restorative discussion as soon as possible with parents present, with a shared vocabulary and structure to work towards a resolution.'

The manner in which the training of the children is at the heart of the change process in the school and the way that those changes have been sustained is significant. No adult wants to be left behind when the children have moved to a better place, after all. What's more, Carr Manor children are now proving to be very adept in not only extolling the benefits of a restorative approach to other schools but actually leading staff training in it. 'We recently took a group of children from Carr Manor to another school,' Simon explained to me, 'where they led a staff training session to help teachers understand more about coaching and restorative practice.'

Of course, in the current climate – in England, at least – no matter how successful a school is, it isn't until it's had the inspectors around to visit. Simon explains: 'In February

2014 Ofsted judged the behaviour and safety at Carr Manor to be "truly outstanding".[4] This could not have happened a while ago.' The report mentions restorative practices – very rare in Ofsted reports – and the short inspection in June 2018 confirms the judgements made in the last full inspection.[5] For Simon, though, this is just a measure of how far they have come not how far they actually go. 'I don't think we've even begun to see what is possible if the children are trusted and encouraged and their relationships are positive and healthy. They are able to be challenged and to support others and the potential feels incredibly strong,' he adds.

WHY CHANGE EFFORTS FAIL

There are many factors that cause change efforts to fail. It could be one big thing (often because another initiative has come along and taken its place) or a combination of variables such as poor timing, lack of support, pressure from external factors, a lack of understanding that the change is necessary, poor leadership, and so on.

When implementation efforts start to fail, organisations can fall into the trap of pointing the finger and then, once the firing squad is established, the blame begins:

- Teachers blame each other and middle leaders.
- Middle leaders blame teachers and senior leaders.
- Senior leaders blame middle leaders and then teachers.

---

4 Ofsted, School Report: Carr Manor Community School (12-13 February 2014), p. 7. Available at: https://files.ofsted.gov.uk/v1/file/2344197.

5 Ofsted, Short Inspection: Carr Manor Community School.

Once the blame game starts it can quickly escalate out of control and it becomes almost impossible to resolve the argument about who did what or who's at fault. The truth is, there is never a winner in these arguments. What is worse is that, once one big idea fails and 'the way we've always done it' bounces back stronger than ever, it makes it even harder to get the next new idea through. If we're not careful, we end up in a situation in which one person's new idea is the whole school's latest fad, a word that has its roots in *fatuus*, the Latin for 'stupid'.

As you would expect having read this far into a book on restorative practice, I always suggest that dialogue is the way forward and that the earlier you can get involved in the life of a problem, the better. Once people have had a chance to say what happened, in their view, and to express how they think and feel about it (remember bubble 1), then it is important to get things back on track as quickly as possible, to refocus on the better future and leave the blemished past behind. A restorative approach is all about focusing your efforts on what you can change (thoughts, behaviours, feelings, the future, and so on) and away from the only thing that you can never change (the past).

Of course, failure isn't the only event that can cause a whole-school project to flounder. Success can be a challenge too. One of the biggest temptations in leading a change effort is to feel that the new ideas are in place and working so, well, my work here is done. Time to move on to the next big idea (or step on the career ladder).

With this in mind, we must work with the guiding team (more on which soon) and across the school on the following:

- Identifying and being explicit about the norms, expectations and values that support the changes.

- Adapting or rewriting key policies and procedures.
- Exploring other training and adapting it to include restorative principles.
- Changing how we recruit new staff.
- Adapting staff induction processes.
- Adapting human resources processes to model ways of working through staff conflict and complaints.
- Adapting governance structures.
- Addressing future development plans.

RELATIONAL LEADERSHIP

In recent years, our understanding of leadership has been distilled through the perspectives of values and, more importantly, relationships. Or, in the words of Simon Sinek:

Leadership isn't about being in charge; it's about taking care of those in your charge.[6]

Today's leaders must be able to identify shared values, co-create a shared vision, create safer spaces, and inspire real collective action. Systems are important, of course, but good restorative leadership never loses sight of the people who make the systems work. They do this by creating a culture and environment that prioritises belonging and a sense of community, grounded in the power of relationships and authentic connection across all teams.

In short, leading people is about the people.

---

6 S. Sinek, Twitter post (28 January 2015). Available at: https://twitter.com/simonsinek/status/560513329148723202?lang=en.

You can't succeed in strategy, practice development or implementing a vision without engaging collaboratively with your teams. We often learn the technical skills needed to undertake improvements and system redesigns; it's less common for us to focus on the deeply relational aspects of effective teamwork. But teams don't just happen. We need to create the conditions to build trust within them and, through this, integrate new ideas, skills and approaches into everyday practice.

Rather than focusing on the impact of the individual – often seen as the 'hero head', an idea beloved of the school turnaround movement, yet an approach that is often proven to be flawed – relational leadership theory focuses on togetherness of and relationships between the individuals and the collective. In doing so, many deeply held assumptions about the nature of leadership are challenged. In particular, notions such as control and independence are interpreted very differently through a relational lens.

So, how is relational leadership cultivated? Well, you won't be surprised to know that it starts with a genuine interest in others. If your ambition to be a head teacher is driven by your love of data, systems and spreadsheets, then a relational approach might not be for you. If being a leader is a humanist vocation for you, then now you're talking. In your school, relationships will be authentically cultivated, there will be a consistent, pervasive focus on empathy and understanding others, and your goal will be to meet staff where *they* are, seeing power and authority (if not accountability) as being shared.

School leaders today are having to confront problems of an unprecedented scale of complexity, from poverty, safeguarding and emotional and mental health matters to the ever-present challenge of name-and-shame accountability measures, high-stakes testing, win-or-lose inspections and direct and indirect political interference to name just a few. While it is true that it is lonely at the top, relational leaders know they are never truly on their own and benefit in no small measure from the time they have invested in building collaborations that count.

RESTORATIVE TEAM AND DEPARTMENT MEETINGS

Of course, we want to practise what we preach, so it makes little sense to make a whole-school shift to restorative approaches if this does not permeate our work as a staff. With that in mind, we are going to want to make sure that all of our staff meetings are restorative. This will also help to build those all-important relationships and the sense of camaraderie and community that is essential to successful whole-school change. The key steps to make this shift happen are as follows:

- Email the team to collect their ideas in order to co-produce a shared agenda – working *with* and not doing *to* or *for*. Remember, emails get responses but going to see colleagues starts a conversation.

- Explore what everyone needs from each other for the meeting to be successful.

- Check in before you begin – remember, connect before content (it applies to colleagues too). Use appropriate check-in questions that are considered and purposeful. Time to talk, to listen and to connect is often missed in the businesses of our roles.

- Ensure there is adequate time to discuss the issues at hand and, importantly, to generate solutions.

- Explore all of the agreed agenda items. If this is not possible, make sure you table the discussion so nothing is written off or forgotten.
- Use solution-focused circles to unlock stuck agenda items.
- Always, always end with a 'Thank you, everyone. Is there anything else we need to say before we close?' Always.
- Use a check-out process. Here are a few ideas for check-in or check-out questions – these are just suggestions. If you think a question is irrelevant or unhelpful at that moment, simply pick another one:
  - Can you introduce yourself and tell us what you prefer to be called?
  - What was your highlight from the weekend?
  - What are you hoping to achieve from today's meeting?
  - When this meeting ends, what's one thing that you are going to do?
  - If you had a day off tomorrow, what would you do and who would you do it with?
  - What's something you've won and how did you win it?
  - What's something that you should throw away, but can't? Explain.
  - What food items did you eat so far today?
  - Who's the most famous person you have met? What famous person would you most like to meet?
  - What kinds of movies do you most enjoy?
  - What was your favourite childhood sweet?

- ▲ What's one thing you are going to take away from this meeting and do differently as a result?
- ▲ Before we close the meeting, can you share three words to describe how you feel the meeting has gone?
- ▲ If we had the chance to hold this meeting again, what would you change about it? Please answer in no more than a sentence.

Of course, a meeting is only as good as its participants – and the expectations and responsibilities of all concerned need to be clear from the outset. Here are seven rules I prepared earlier:

1. Meetings are owned by all and it is everyone's responsibility to make them successful.
2. They take place in a circle.
3. There are no passengers, only crew.
4. A meeting should always start with the check-in process and end with a check-out.
5. Attendance is non-negotiable (unless agreed otherwise with a line manager prior to the meeting).
6. Taking of minutes and facilitating is done on a rota basis.
7. No one should lose sight of the fact that this is a team-focused event and that relationship building, even when there are disagreements, is key.

GUIDING TEAM

Senior leadership teams cannot implement change in isolation, they need other willing colleagues. The success of the whole-school approach largely depends on the quality of the guiding team – the team created to monitor and help implement sustainable change around a particular project – and the importance the leadership places upon it. This is something that is often missed and can lead to wasted efforts.

The senior leadership team must create the right conditions and a set of permissions, and give that group enough organisational power to lead the change effort and keep it on target through its various stages. The group must contain some senior leaders but be made up of a cross-section of staff from across teaching and learning, pastoral care and business support, with regular input from parents, carers and children. Here, in true restorative fashion, we are talking about being in the *with* box.

That said, senior leaders must resist the temptation to stack the team with just those staff they can most easily free up. Every member of the team must be there for a reason: they need to be able to propel the group forward. An effective guiding team has the right mix of individuals at different levels of the organisation. They will need to be:

- Naturally relational. While restorative practice may be new to them, restorative thinking probably isn't.

- Quick to pick up expertise in – and willing to model – working restoratively.

- Authoritative enough to drive the change. They don't have to be a senior leader, but they must have leadership skills.

- Diverse. Diversity is essential: diversity in thinking, diversity in culture, diversity in approach.
- Credible among their peers.
- Able to leverage talent across the school when needed.
- Able to challenge and support at all levels of the organisation. That's high challenge and high support, remember. That's doing things *with*.

Have one member of the group who acts as a critical friend. They should be just a bit further along the scepticism spectrum – not enough that it sucks the life out of people, meetings and implementation efforts, but just enough to choose their moments to tactfully question how things are going. Senior leaders must stay involved with the group throughout the change effort and invite feedback about what's happening, as well as feed back to the group about what they are hearing across the school.

PRACTICE DEVELOPMENT GROUPS

Ongoing and intensive professional development, which includes building skills around restorative conversations, should be provided for all staff. This professional development needs to happen throughout the year and should be paired with action learning coaching sessions, which help to move theory into practice. Professional development should be responsive to school needs at the beginning of the new school year and revisited at various points. The ultimate goal is about moving practice to the point of conscious competence – you are able to do it, but only when you think about it – and, from there to unconscious competence – you just do it because, well, that's how we do things around here.

I suggest delivering training through approaches that are designed to deliver skills-based learning that will promote and embed practice. Training should be based on the action-learning principles of questioning, reflecting and building on current strengths. In short, doing things *with* people, rather than *to* or *for* them. Training should always model restorative principles to assist participants in clarifying group protocols, giving direct input and facilitating group reflection. The approach to learning will be a combination of presentations, interactive discussions and group and personal exercises. The emphasis will be on engagement and using the skills and knowledge of the whole group.

We should really think about stopping all one-off training and only invest in long-term programmes with taught, practical and reflective elements which are linked to the overarching organisational strategy for practice development. The ideal model of training, based on my experience, starts with leadership and key groups of staff meeting initially for an extended twilight or as part of an INSET day, which will provide an introduction to the key principles of restorative practice, including the importance of relationships and the power of working *with*. This can be followed by modules of action learning to develop skills, identify what good practice is and share experiences in collaboration with others.

These modules should cover what I think are the most important basics when it comes to a move to relational practice in schools:

- Developing a restorative mindset (including how we look at the school culture and at our relationships across the community).

- Restorative conversations and language.
- Using circles.
- Holding meetings differently and dealing with conflict, including more formal processes.
- Practice sustainability.

You'll notice that this book covers each of these points, so hopefully this will be a useful starting point in planning your training around restorative practice.

WHO ARE THE CHAMPIONS?

Every project needs champions and any school looking at a culture shift towards a restorative model would do well to identify, support and, yes, cherish theirs. A school should seek to build the knowledge, skills and passion for restorative practice in those who will champion, model and support others. In turn, the role of these champions is to provide peers with a deeper level of understanding and experience of the philosophy and techniques of restorative practice, and to promote a greater awareness of relational working.

Senior leaders will need to develop the champions' mindsets and confidence so that they will be able to model restorative practice in their teaching and in their work with colleagues. When they embody the principles of restorative practice, they can seek to support individuals to recognise different behavioural approaches and see how to change their practice.

So, to sum up, the benefits of champions are:

- Increased motivation and skill for using restorative practice in the champion's own team and area.
- A source of support and modelling of restorative practice and approaches.
- Increased project capacity for briefing teams on restorative practice, facilitating circles, delivering informal awareness sessions, facilitating restorative conversations, and so on.
- Greater awareness of restorative practice in action and the impact this is having in the school.
- Reduced duplication of effort and resources.
- Improved staff performance, morale and relationships.
- Increased use of restorative practice across the school, with increased individual responsibility and mutually respectful challenge. Creating the space for staff and leaders to sit together and have honest and open conversations which create powerful feedback loops from staff to leaders and back to staff.
- Capacity to evaluate what's working well and what would be better if …

TRAINING STUDENTS

Getting it right with the adults in the school first is crucial to ensuring that we have the optimal model for our students to follow. However, if we want the change to be embedded in the fabric of the school, we need to train the students too.

Conflict is a normal part of life and, one way or another, students often resolve issues on their own. A fight behind the bike sheds is one way of resolving conflict, after all. However, sometimes they will need help to do this more effectively and maturely. Given the choice, they may even prefer these conflicts to be resolved among peers rather than with a staff member. Indeed, when I train secondary school students in restorative approaches, it is always clear that they feel their peers will understand them better after an incident and that they think they will be less likely to get into trouble if they open up to their peers. This is not about eschewing punishment but means that they will at least feel listened to, so the focus can be more on putting things right going forward than on simply doling out sanctions.

When it comes to upskilling children and young people in restorative schools, they can be trained as peer mentors or peer mediators, but I prefer seeing them trained in the same way as staff. In this way, we highlight the manner in which whole-school change is about working together for everyone's benefit, something that is reinforced by everyone doing similar training and using the same language and content, with only slight adaptation for context. Don't think that this is something just for older children either. I have trained children as young as six or seven in restorative practice. We should never underestimate what they are capable of when properly trained and supported and when they see great role models in the adults around them.

In one primary school I worked with, they trained children to help out at play times and lunchtimes. They befriend children who are on their own, proactively work with peers and, when low-level arguments or friendship fallouts happen, give their time to support the protagonists in understanding the impact their behaviours have on each other and then facilitate dialogue so they can find resolutions. While we need to be fully aware of our safeguarding responsibilities around what students can and can't help with – and ensure that they know when to pass an issue to the relevant adults – training students in restorative practice gives them opportunities to learn real skills which will last them a lifetime.

I also think it's important to introduce them to the basics and key principles of restorative practice through their day-to-day classroom experiences, tutor groups, assemblies, and more focused sessions if the timetable permits. In this way, they are consistently receiving the message that this is not something that just the adults do; it's something we all do. For example, one school I worked with in Knowsley set aside ten minutes, once a week in staff meetings and in classrooms, for everyone to share their 'tweak of the week'. In this way, they were focusing on one small aspect of restorative practice – a 1% gain, as we discussed earlier – as a way of getting the whole community up to speed.

Children need to be crew, not passengers – as we've seen – and training them up to be as competent as the adults in restorative practice goes a long way to achieving that. And then what? Well, imagine a world in which conflict in and between communities can be effectively managed by the people in those communities themselves.

FINAL THOUGHTS

I wish you the best of luck as you set out on your journey into restorative practice. Yes, change can be challenging, but I hope that I've convinced you that the destination is worth seeking. Here is a final list of pointers to help guide you on the way.

A LIST OF THINGS TO REMEMBER – SOME SMALL AND SOME A BIT BIGGER

- All behaviour is an unmet need.
- Connect before content.
- Create a sense of belonging.
- Follow the 1% principle.
- Empathy isn't sympathy.
- Make regular deposits into the 'social capital' bank.
- Strike when the iron's cold.
- Culture exists in every organisation – is yours by design or by default?
- Know your children (and their families) well and allow them to know you well too.
- Every child (and adult) needs a champion.
- Don't be afraid of the 'L word' – spread it thick like my mum spreads butter.

- If you're not modelling what you're teaching, you're not teaching what you think you're teaching.
- Labels belong on jars.
- Involve families in creating a dream team.
- Don't forget significant and important others.
- Aim for high challenge and high support.
- You can't put students first if you put teachers last.
- Relationship policy before behaviour policy.
- Set meetings up to succeed.
- Learn from Carr Manor Community School's example.
- Build bridges, not brick walls.
- The restorative chat is everyone's friend.
- It's not a script, it's a structure.
- You need more questions and fewer answers.
- The restorative five.
- The three bubbles.
- Everything looks better when you put it in a circle.
- Set up the seats.
- Craft the right questions.
- Prepare for circles to succeed.
- Use solution-focused circles.
- One size doesn't fit all; in fact, it only ever fits one.
- Evaluate existing systems.
- Make your team and department meetings restorative.

FINAL THOUGHTS

- Follow the five steps to success.
- Think about how to make change stick.
- Guide the team.
- Find your champions.
- Train the students.

REFERENCES AND FURTHER READING

Augustine, C. H., Engberg, J., Grimm, G. E., Lee, E., Lin Wang, E., Christianson, K. and Joseph, A. A. (2018) *Can Restorative Practices Improve School Climate and Curb Suspensions? An Evaluation of the Impact of Restorative Practices in a Mid-Sized Urban School District* (Santa Monica, CA: RAND Corporation). Available at: https://www.rand.org/pubs/research_reports/RR2840.html.

Block, P. (2008) *Community: The Structure of Belonging* (San Francisco, CA: Berrett-Koehler Publishers).

Bonell, C., Allen, E., Warren, E., McGowan, J., Bevilacqua, L., Jamal, F., Legood, R., Wiggins, M., Opondo, C., Mathiot, A., Sturgess, J., Fletcher, A., Sadique, Z., Elbourne, D., Christie, D., Bond, L., Scott, S. and Viner, R. M. (2018) Effects of the Learning Together Intervention on Bullying and Aggression in English Secondary Schools (INCLUSIVE): A Cluster Randomised Controlled Trial, *Lancet* 392: 2452–2464.

Brown, B. (2010) *The Gifts of Imperfection: Let Go of Who You Think You're Supposed to Be and Embrace Who You Are* (Center City, MN: Hazelden Publishing).

Brown, B. (2013) *Daring Greatly: How the Courage to Be Vulnerable Transforms the Way We Live, Love, Parent, and Lead* (London: Penguin).

Christie, N. (1977) Conflicts as Property, *The British Journal of Criminology* 17(1): 1–15. Available at: https://academic.oup.com/bjc/article/17/1/1/411623.

Covey, S. R. (2004) *The 7 Habits of Highly Effective People: Powerful Lessons in Personal Change* (New York: Simon & Schuster).

Dweck, C. S. (2014) The Power of Yet [video], *TEDxNorrköping* (12 September). Available at: https://www.youtube.com/watch?v=J-swZaKN2Ic.

Dzur, A. (2016) Conversations on Restorative Justice: A Talk with Tim Chapman, *Restorative Justice* 4(1): 115–129.

Gallo, P. (2016) Why Positive Relationships at Work Matter More Than You Think, *World Economic Forum* (16 March). Available at: https://www.weforum.org/agenda/2016/03/why-positive-relationships-are-key-to-real-success-at-work/.

Gilbert, I. (2007) *The Little Book of Thunks: 260 Questions to Make Your Brain Go Ouch!* (Carmarthen: Crown House Publishing).

Goddard, V. (2014) *The Best Job in the World* (Carmarthen: Independent Thinking Press).

Glaser, Daniel (1969) *The Effectiveness of a Prison and Parole System* (Indianapolis, IN: Bobbs-Merrill).

Guardian, The (2013) Barack Obama's Address at Nelson Mandela's Memorial Service – in Full (10 December). Available at: https://www.theguardian.com/world/2013/dec/10/barack-obama-nelson-mandela-memorial-service.

Johnson, S. (1999) *Who Moved My Cheese? An Amazing Way to Deal with Change in Your Work and in Your Life* (London: Vermilion).

Kohli, R. and Solórzano, D. G. (2012) Teachers, Please Learn Our Names! Racial Microagressions and the K–12 Classroom, *Race Ethnicity and Education* 15(4): 441–462, DOI: 10.1080/13613324.2012.674026.

Kotter, J. and Rathgeber, H. (2006) *Our Iceberg Is Melting: Changing and Succeeding Under Any Conditions* (London: Macmillan).

Lewis, T. (2019) Golden Aura Around Marginal Gains Is Beginning to Look a Little Tarnished, *The Guardian* (20 October). Available at: https://www.theguardian.com/sport/blog/2019/oct/20/marginal-gains-tarnished-bradley-wiggins-dave-brailsford.

Lundin, S. and Nelson, B. (2010) *Ubuntu! An Inspiring Story About an African Tradition of Teamwork and Collaboration* (New York: Broadway Books).

REFERENCES AND FURTHER READING

National Scientific Council on the Developing Child (2004) *Young Children Develop in an Environment of Relationships*. Working Paper No. 1 (Cambridge, MA: Harvard University Center on the Developing Child). Available at: https://developingchild.harvard.edu/wp-content/uploads/2004/04/Young-Children-Develop-in-an-Environment-of-Relationships.pdf.

O'Connell, T. (1998) *Conferencing Handbook: The New Real Justice Training Manual* (Pipersville, PA: The Piper's Press).

O'Connell, T. (2000) *Restorative Justice for Police: Foundations for Change*. Paper presented at the United Nations Crime Congress, Ancillary Meeting on Implementing Restorative Justice in the International Context. Vienna, Austria (10–17 April). Available at: http://restorativejustice.org/10fulltext/oconnell.

Ofsted (2014) School Report: Carr Manor Community School (12–13 February). Available at: https://files.ofsted.gov.uk/v1/file/2344197.

Ofsted (2018) Short Inspection: Carr Manor Community School, Specialist Sports College (26 June). Available at: https://files.ofsted.gov.uk/v1/file/2786537.

Poole, G. (2003) *The Complete Book of Questions: 1001 Conversation Starters for Any Occasion* (Grand Rapids, MI: Zondervan).

Rosenberg, M. B. (1999) *Nonviolent Communication: A Language of Compassion* (Encinitas, CA: PuddleDancer Press).

RSA (2013) Brené Brown on Empathy [video] (10 December). Available at: https://www.youtube.com/watch?v=1Evwgu369Jw.

Skinns, L., Du Rose, N. and Hough, M. (2009) *An Evaluation of Bristol RAiS* (London: Institute for Criminal Policy Research and King's College London). Available at: https://restorativejustice.org.uk/sites/default/files/resources/files/Bristol%20RAiS%20full%20report.pdf.

Slater, M. (2012) Olympics Cycling: Marginal Gains Underpin Team GB Dominance, *BBC Sport* (8 August). Available at: https://www.bbc.co.uk/sport/olympics/19174302.

Thompson, F. and Smith, P. K. (2011) *The Use and Effectiveness of Anti-Bullying Strategies in Schools*. Research Report DFE-RR098 (London: Department for Education).

Wachtel, J. (2009) Toward Peace and Justice in Brazil: Dominic Barter and Restorative Circles, *IIRP News* (20 March). Available at: https://www.iirp.edu/news/toward-peace-and-justice-in-brazil-dominic-arter-and-restorative-circles.

Wachtel, T. and McCold, P. (2008) Restorative Justice in Everyday Life. In H. Strang and J. Braithwaite (eds), *Restorative Justice and Civil Society* (Cambridge: Cambridge University Press), pp. 114–129.

INDEPENDENT THINKING ON …

MFL
978-178135337-0

RESTORATIVE PRACTICE
978-178135338-7

TEACHING AND LEARNING
978-178135339-4

TRANSITION
978-178135340-0

LAUGHTER
978-178135341-7

TEACHING IN HIGHER EDUCATION
978-178135369-1

EMOTIONAL LITERACY
978-178135373-8

LOSS
978-178135353-0

independent thinking press

www.independentthinkingpress.com

independent thinking

Independent Thinking. An education company.

Taking people's brains for a walk since 1994.

We use our words.

www.independentthinking.com